photos by a.d. camera

Using modern-day tools like image generating computers the graphic engineers apply new methods and otherwise challenge obsolete techniques to gain wider audiences for their works. By all means necessary they utilize marketing instruments like magazines, old-fashioned target-prop style posters and even stickers to attract attention. On the other hand they attempt seriously to maintain an authentic low profile. The urge to venture into further regions takes the graphic pioneers to other platforms besides the usual exhibition and gallery circus. 25 years old Marok, is constantly questioning media standards with an innovative magazine. With his lense Eddie Otchere captures up-coming HipHop and Drum'n'Bass acts, while Evan Hecox and Andy Howell illustrate skate- and snowboarding supply, In addition to their regular graphic art these prolific pro performers frequently adapt their skills to related projects. Futura 2000 in designing toy-robots, HAZE in manufacturing furniture. BLK/MRKT's team mates are postering the streets with intriguing propaganda material. The artistic entrepreneurs have a single activity in common. The most usual modification of this all condition art: the fabrication of endurance wear for concrete action and clubculture.
The art is on everything.
This compilation by Lodown Magazine's Finest, publisher and artdirector Thomas Marecki aka Marok and Photographer Alex Flach aka Flachfotografix, is a further extension of this media-savvy visual output. Consequently, it's the common intention to popularize this art form, to guarantee the easy access for everyone. Sounds like the remixed Bauhaus-esque demand for function transporting form combined with simple reproducible materials and the highly acclaimed theorem 'everything is art' of 6oies screenprinting art. Contemplating this essential and compelling statement the sample communication art featured on the following pages represents the modernized sequel to Pop Art. Hence it is Post-Pop-Pre-Shrink-Art. Or whatsoever... Give it a name.

Nevertheless, that's the lowdown on it. Without any hype intended.
by a. hesse

Metropolitan areas, crowded cityscapes, centered in downtown. Right here inner city life comes with a pacing up-tempo, permanently in flux. This demanding environment has a major influence on its juvenile inhabitants, emerging a stunning versatility coping with the urban impressions. Grafitti as urban youth's signature is added to municipal traffic signs and advertising. Gradually, skateboarding became the most efficient transport system. HipHop tracks and Drum'n'Bass tunes set the arhythmetic urban sounds to music.

introducing; **lodown graphic engineering**

Concerning this massive impact on one's adolescence this book's protagonists have developed their individual mode of expression. Maneuvering through your sourrounding on a skateboard creates a different perception on architecture and facilities. Concrete serves as an intriguing playground, overcoming obstacles like curbs and handrails with the wooden toy. You learn how to read your hometown, noticing fragmentary aerosol throw-ups.

It's the street art of cryptic graffiti, still indicating HipHop's presence in your neighborhood, that took various gifted writers to other artforms, like painting, graphic art or product design. Coming straight from the underground, these graphic young'uns depicted in this compilation use all different parts of their creative background resulting in their own unique interpretation of contemporary art. Concluding in utterly distinguished versions the creative process of each featured artist is similar to sampling, editing, dubbing and remixing in present time computer-based music.
Refering to a digital renaissance of eccelctisism all available units of photography and typeface were dismembered and rephrased in a new kind of context to paraphrase and construct an improved upshot. Repeating old achievements. Inserting to advanced definitions. Though these distracting elements of visuals and fonts converge symbiotically into a visual track, the artists focus on the visual appearance to emphasize the subliminal reflection of the their asscoiated fields. Thereby they avoid the visual monotony caused by exclusively arbitrary alteration of typography.

[lodown]

LODOWN MAG

boarding, thrills & entertainment

numero uno . still summer 95 issue .

rocks da house numero uno . still summer 95 issue .

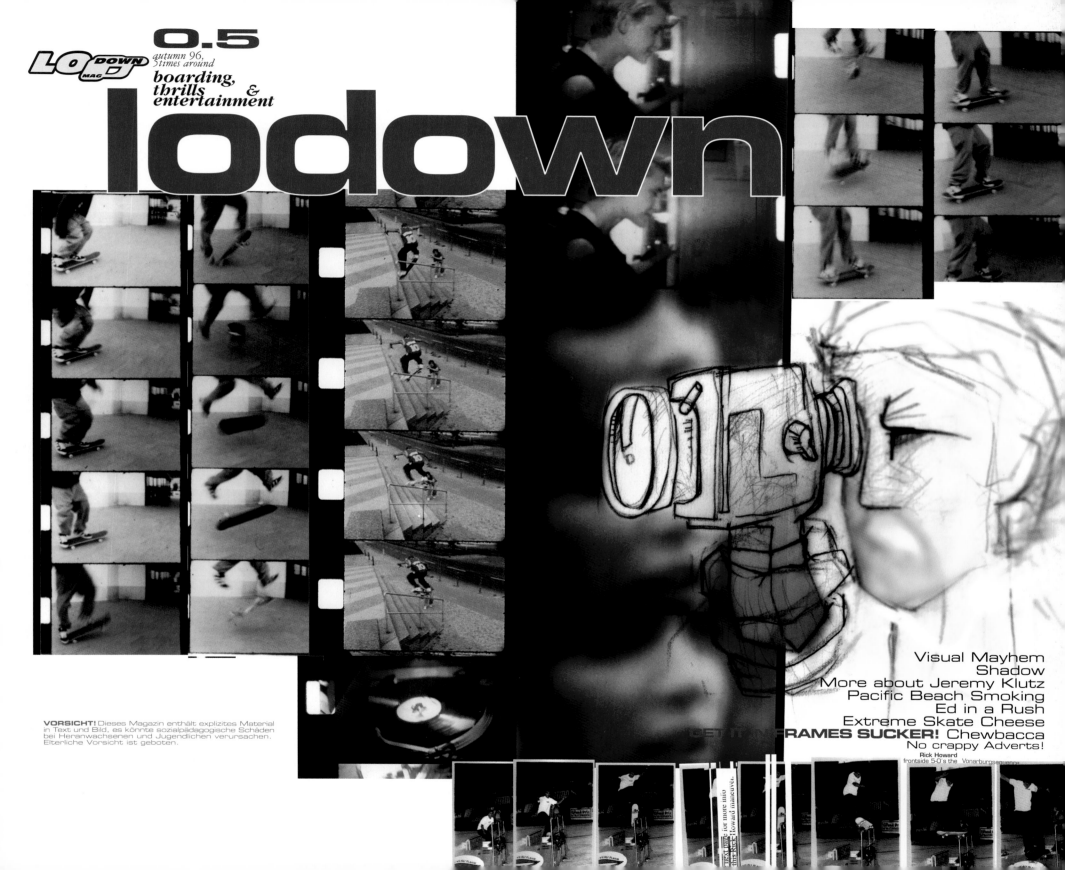

lodown

LODOWN MAG

0.5

*autumn 96,
3 times around*

**boarding,
thrills &
entertainment**

VORSICHT! Dieses Magazin enthält explizites Material in Text und Bild, es könnte sozialpädagogische Schäden bei Heranwachsenen und Jugendlichen verursachen. Elterliche Vorsicht ist geboten.

Visual Mayhem
Shadow
More about Jeremy Klutz
Pacific Beach Smoking
Ed in a Rush
Extreme Skate Cheese
GET IT IN FRAMES SUCKER! Chewbacca
No crappy Adverts!

Rick Howard
frontside 5-0's the Vonarburgsequence

LO·DOWN

boarding,
thrills &
entertainment

spring96

*this mag is absolutely not
political correct ! It's dealing
with Sex, Drugs and heavy
Stunts. Parents be aware!*

ESCAPE

FROM URBAN DISASTER SOCIETIES

SLAM!

Lodown presents
**"Great Moments in the
History of Skateboarding"**

Collectors edition part #1

An impressive Airkoston
indyflips his board to victory.
Lausanne Grand Prix 96.
Koston takes the title.
Real slammin', man!

MUNICIPAL LODOWN TRAINING COUNCIL COMBAT TARGET

SCORE SHADED AREA K5 ONL

To score duel target combat course add the total of K5's on both targets.

TOTAL IMPACT

9 in the clip and one in the chamber for all you punkmotherfuckers tryin' to get the corporate gripon. *sound. concret. snow. art & entertainment.* +superlo8poster
usuals.

IN-TRO 009

lonely heart slide

we connect:

in order of appearance: stuntwoodriders in motion, skiboarding enthusiastics, sonic sound challengers, lo-fi percussionists, rappers on cocain, artistic and autistic verbalism, abstract concrete visualists, all condition ecclecticism, cinematic helmers, homophobic nazis for jesus christ, post pop preshrink art, threethousand, metropolitan retro guerilla technics, pioneering dual teleturntableism, cipher logicalists, advanced premillenium sociological research, disposable antifuck, innovative fakie maneuvers, hertha enlargement, sampleopportunism, dubbed rephrasing in one incredible magazine.
we are so far out, it's dark here.

=>>>the buttomline is: **don't fuck around with us!**

=>>>sequence is: **marcus jürgensen extra prolific on a ninestair skoolyard rail.** pic. macca

intro: **suckers still suck!**
we're sorry 'bout that.

INFORMATIONMANIPULATION.
WHO FILTRATES THE INFINITY
OF OUR COSMOS. DEFINES USELESS
INFORMATION AND MEDIAHYPES WILL
USELESS DEFINITIONS OF ABSTRACT
OPINIONS. WE DONT NEED TO BE
GUIDED. YOU NEVER TOUCH OUR
DIMENSIONS. BUT YOU CAN
SCRATCH & SNIFF YOU
SUCKIN' BITCH!

00 11 22
33 44 5
66 77 88
99? !!!'::
$ £ Æ Ø
& ¡¡ ((¦ ' ''

UNLAWFUL FLIGHT TO AVID PROSECUTION - AGGRAVATED MURDER, ATTEMPTED MURDER

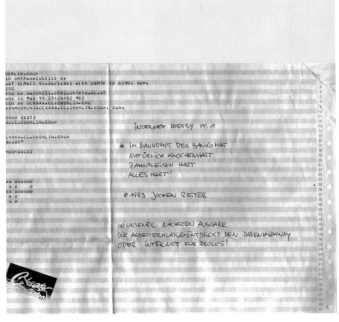

INTERNET POETRY PT. 1

* IN BANKOMAT DER BANKOMAT
NATÜRLICH KNOCHENHART
ZAHNFLEISCH HART
ALLES HART!

© 1983 JOCHEN REITER

IN UNSERER NÄCHSTEN AUSGABE:
DIE ARBEITERKLASSE ENTDECKT DEN DATENHIGHWAY
ODER INTERNET FÜR PROLOS!

left to right: **'informationmanipulation'**, poetry by **cheapentertainment**, **'crackgrinder'**
opposite: **'loose fit sam'**

sam, the fame, and the brothers grim.

sicks.

we are sick...
sick of all those faggots speaking up, coz they got some money to spend in the mediajungle of corruptness. biting is all that today, but if you bite, please take it to another level.
we are sick of cheap imitators sucking styles and milking it to death. -please calm down.

...this issue fits,

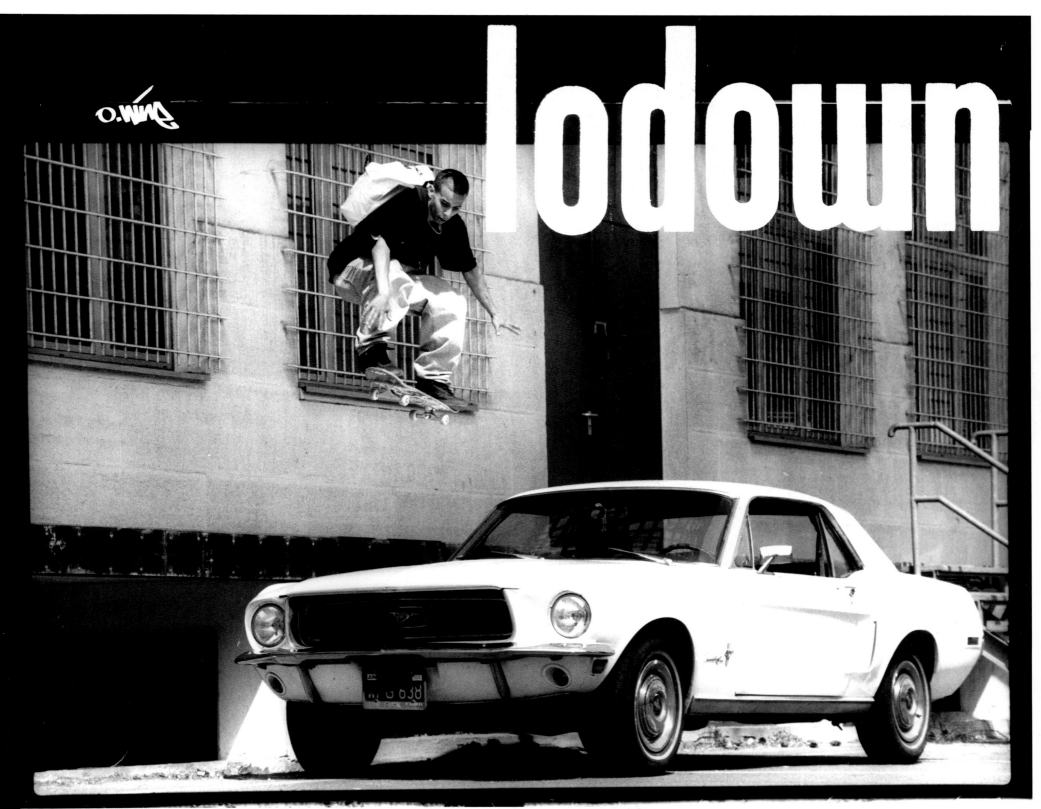

lodown

sami harithi ollies over the lodownwheels on cover no. nine, oliver wia photo opposite: the brothers grim intro sicks

Once it started with a little piece of wood. It happened to be his first skateboard. A green one, shaped like a frog, given to him by his parents. Just a regular present to a regular little kid? Definitely not. Sami's life changed immediately and forever. Developing an individual perception of his surroundings, he conquered his hometown Berlin. Day in, day out Sami spent his time on his skateboard, formerly just known to him as this little piece of wood. Due to his dedication and creativity Sam became one of the most influential and innovative athletes in European skateboarding, highly acclaimed for his unique style, and the ability to skate anything and everything - constantly on the move.

Soon, right after turning twelve, he was already sponsored by Powell Peralta, at this time Powell was the industry's leading company. He was one of the first European skateboarders featured in an American skatevideo. His concrete maneuvers fascinated many people including his brother. Sami's influence made him start skateboarding.

Berlin was on the map of international skateboarding, He lead an young and fearless group of talented and gifted skateboarders all around Europe, pushing the physical boundaries to the level no one ever witnessed in Europe before, presenting this sport of individuality and expression to a new and by far wider audience. Afterwards he hooked up with skatelegend Tony Hawk's rising company Birdhouse. In '93 he teamed up with the Birdhouse crew including his American match Willie Santos for a demo tour troughout the United States. Back in the Old World he claimed two European Championchips, several international titles and countless video appearances. Finally, he ended up with an other sponsor, Huntington Beach based Flip Skateboards. (Changing companies is an ordinary procedure in skateboarding, not to be considered as a form of cheating your former mentors.)

Skateboarding puts Sami onto higher levels in life. He moved several times to different people and to different countries, got used to other people and opened his personality to other themes in life, which him may allows to deal with problems in an advanced and humble manner.

So Skateboarding isn't about useless wooden toys anymore. Skateboarding gave him the opportunity to live the life everybody is dreaming.

Nowadays, he is on his board for more then a decade, things have changed. It is time to move on, to take the next step and progress. Skateboarding is bigger then ever before and it is Sam's choice to make a living out of it.
Ride on!

sami harithi

When you meet him take a minute and watch him doing the hardest tricks with an easy flow and an unique style. The raddest maneuvers look so easy and motivates and enjoys everybody.
Even if Sami's feet didn't touch his board he is pure entertainment.

fuck the intro. this is the content. it contains a stolen
moment of sami's life, swinging over a doubleset.

flachfotog.

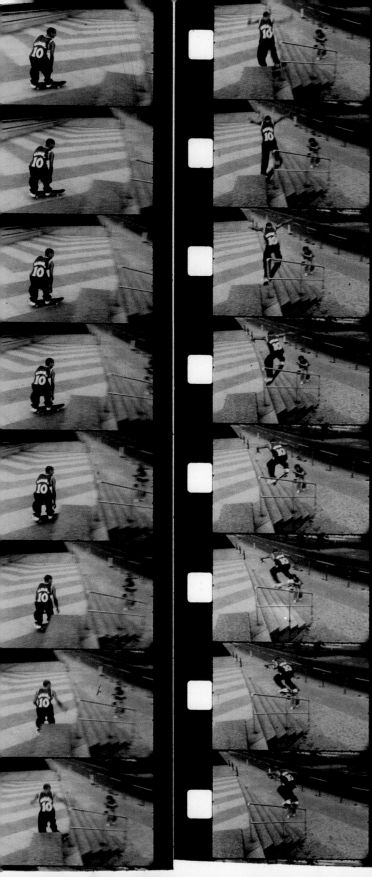

GIMME5

>> Enough!<<

context

it seems that sam has taken over these pages. congratulations, sam!
50-50 captured on reel

a.d. camera

AS SEEN ON
TV

sami harithi - professional skateboarder

"superbreak"

huge ollie over the V8 engine with a pocket full of kryptonite
during principal photography for a commercial in '97

sam shows no fear to jump in front of
some ladies. gap ollie at the
kunstgewerbemuseum in berlin in '96

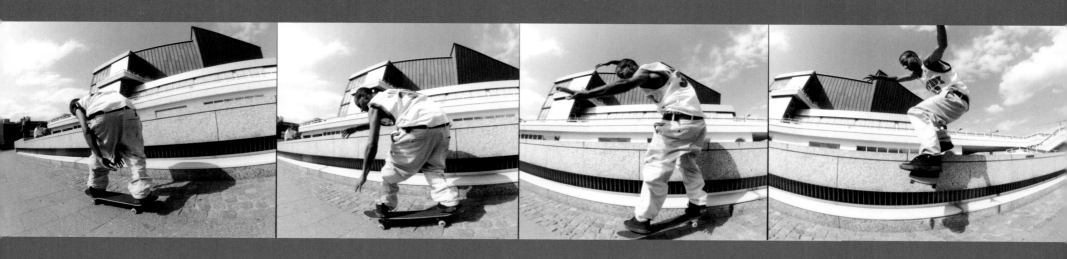

sami's slide show at the berlin philharmonie

top: backside 180 kickflip
middle: tailslide to fakie
bottom: switchstance frontside 180 ollie
all moves performed at the kunstforum

a sequence of sam executing a frontside 180
ollie on a dark and rainy day

Sami playing with the camera, his board, a handrail
and a set of stairs
performed for a europe vans advert campagne in '97

SAMI HARITHI

top-sequence: **b.s. 180 kickflip**
below-sequence: **f.s. 180 ollie to backward nosewheelie**
both tricks were executed at the philharmonie

WE MUST VENTURE INTO THE UNKNOWN DARKNESS.

sam consults dr. octagon...

clockwise whole spread:
till kemner grinds a rail in downtown berlin,
the nationalposse representing at the nationalgallery,
robert stoye, frontside boardslides to shovit, a bench in the former american sector,
the brandenburg gate,
murmel pops a fat backside 180 ollie at the historic berlin milestone,
sequence: noisy frontside 50-50 under the tentacles of the metropolitan transport system

BERLIN-RUNDSCHAU

ge wirken für die Skatebordfahrer wie Adrenalin: „Du willst hoch, höher und höher. Du willst deine Grenzen sehen und sie überwinden."

Foto: Kalazois

Sprünge wirken für die Skatebordfahrer wie Adrenalin: „Du willst hoch, höher und höher. Du willst deine Grenzen sehen und sie überwinden."

Auf Rollen brettern sie ziellos durch die Stadt

Berlins Skateboardfahrer sind im Winter ohne Heimat / V

Verbote an den interessante Plätzen

berlin represents

LODOWN

sequence: **till's** nosegrinding to fakie at this thirdeyeoptic pyramid near the 'palast der republik',
formerly known as the playground of the phony parliament of the east german republic,
small picture: smith grind,
sequence opposite: a real act of balance. backside 50-50, 180 off,
big picture: late night skateboarding is fun because you can use spots like the one till is grinding at
the daytime overcrowded ku-damm

clockwise starting left:
stickorama 5-0's the opel-handrails by jonn rübke,
basti nosegrinding a bench,
the latest entry to berlin population, **chris heitmann**,
flipping his board down stairs and over a bench at
'frankfurter allee', ex-russian sector,
murderdeathkills 187 berlin, **lodown tribute to marzahn
robert** uses contempory architecture to catch some
airplay at the 'kulturforum',
a berlin visitor, **patrick ehling**, backside 50-50's a
handrail

sequence: **timo pritzel** hurls his body down a cliff in the concrete jungle near the nationalgallery

ali b. handling his bike in all different variations with pride, at the 'lighthall' at berlins technical university

darryl's page
clockwise starting right:
freeze, you little flying stepper!
umd ad campaign, photographed at the lighthall,
headspining darryl in a subway-station.

one for the trouble,
two for hard times....

Boyscouts Paradise

VERSARY SPECIAL

Boyscouts, I
think this
woman needs
our help.

Do you think
she is ill?

I don't know,
but maybe she
is hurt.

Or dead?

SA DREIKANT & SHELLEY MASTERS
BUNCH OF SIX-CRAZED UBERFRAUEN™ AND LAME SK8-CRAP
EST BUDDIES AT ABUSE INDUSTRIES™

Abuse Industries

graphics vs. product
5 directions

Eric Haze...................(of Haze
Ed Templeton.....(of Toy Machine
John Grigley.........(of Old Ghosts
Eli Bonerz................(of X-Large
Erik Brunetti.)................(of Fuct
Zero One Gallery

7025 Melrose Avenue
June 21 - August 20 1997
Opening Reception June 21, 7 -11 p.m.

futura's last entry

THI CHOSEN BROTHA·
USING SUPERIOR
CREATIVITY·TOGETHER WITH

LO DOWN MAG
DS

Shepard Fairey. What started out eight years ago as a private joke for a Rhode Island School of Design student (and his skateboarding friends) has since snowballed into something of a minor cultural phenomenom. Shepard´s One-Man Army is responsible for all those "Andre The Giant Has A Posse" stickers plastered throughout cities like Providence, Boston, New York, Philly, San Diego, San Francisco, Paris, London, Vienna, and Tokyo. They also adorn traffic lights, mailboxes, and stop signs in even more remote areas of the globe.
His designs depict the sallow-faced wrestler moonlighting as other celebrities - Jimi Hendrix, Neil Armstrong, Sid Vicious, Gene Simmons, and Ringo Starr, among others - as well as ad campaigns like the "Okay Soda" spoof. In New England, imitations/commentaries are limited only by other artists' imaginations. For him, his joke has been transformed into a semi-serious socio-psychological experiment with the masses, and if other artists want to comment on it, that's fine with him. It's all a reaction to, and commentary on, pop culture.

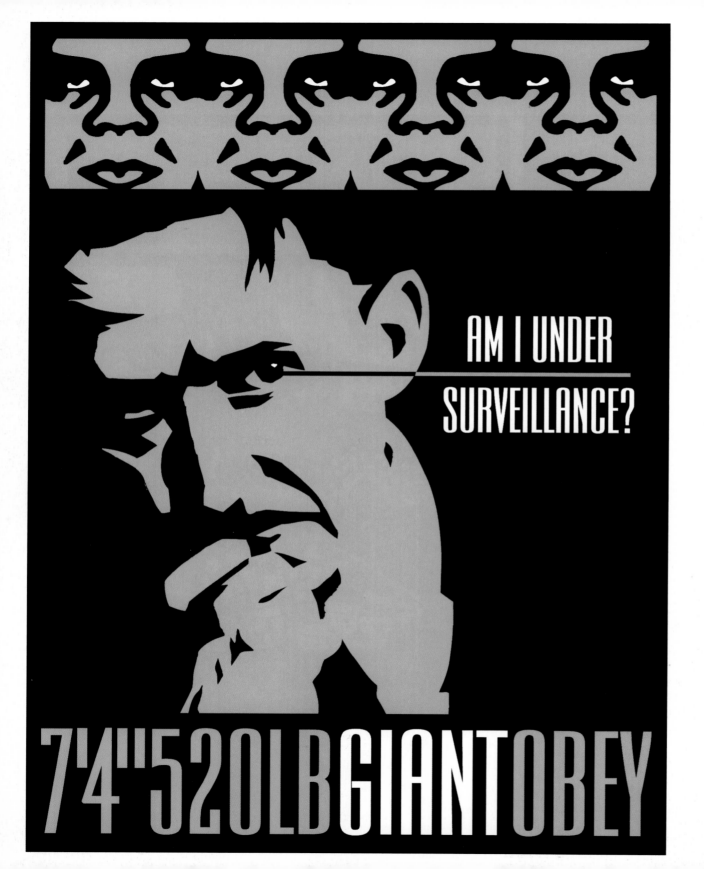

AM I UNDER
SURVEILLANCE?

7'4"520LBGIANTOBEY

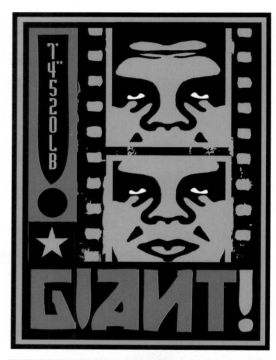

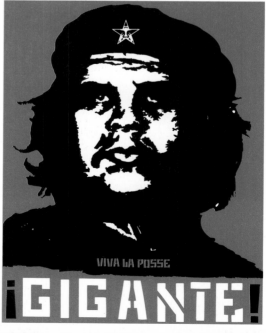

BLK/MRKT (BLACK MARKET): a contradiction in the corporate design world. A collection of underground artists (and ideals) working to create an innovative design firm. From the "Andre the Giant has a posse" sticker/poster campaign to graffitti to painting to fine-art web installations, this design team has it covered. Rather than bringing the underground to the surface, Black Market Creative Visual Communications works to blur the distinctions, to attack everything with the same attitude: guerrilla marketing on a corporate scale.

I'D RATHER DIE THAN REVEAL THE SECRET OF MY ART!

BLK/MRKT
BLACK MARKET CREATIVE VISUAL COMMUNICATION

BLK/MRKT
CREATIVE VISUAL COMMUNICATION

Shepard Fairey

Dave Kinsey

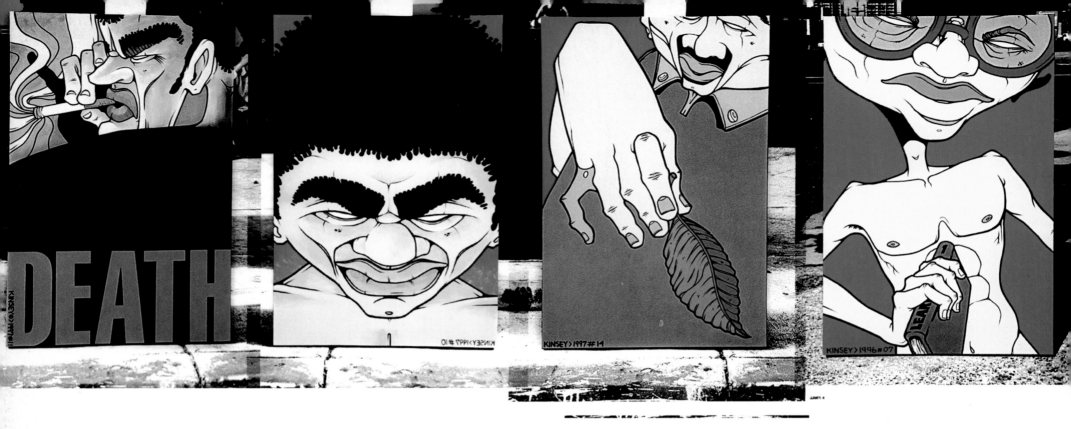

Dave Kinsey is busy developing chair-butt from all the time spent in front of his computer, but we like to think it's worth it. He can do five t-shirt designs in the same time I can get upset, rip one up, throw it in the trash and start over again. He has designed and art directed for companies like Droors Clothing, DC Shoes, Tree Fort Skateboards, Dub Weathergear, Blunt Snowboard Magazine and now Black Market. Maybe his years at the Art Institute of Atlanta, where he got his degree, have paid off. Now, in his own time, he paints and comes up with new promotional ideas for Black Market. His past as a graffitti artist and traditional painter have also paid off, helping to set Black Market's portfolio apart.

con·sump·tion (kən-sŭmp′shən) n. 1. The act or process of comsuming. 2. The using up of consumer goods or services. 3. To waste: *as in taking more than one needs to survive.*

ex·tin·guish (ĭk-stĭng′gwĭsh) v. 1.To put out (a flame or fire). 2. To put to an end; destroy: *as in extermination of a particular creature.*

EXTINGUISH

CONSUMPTION

The art and design Jose Gomez

IN.

NOW.

BLINDED

T 10 TIMES

FROM

DERSTAND

und das

TSKATE

five-o grind

CF

15 34

RHYTHM

I have a good friend named **Jose Gomez**, but I call him Pepito. He's one of the most creative people I know, a real artist in the truest sense. Jose has never worried about the superficial things our institutional society pushes on us, he lives in his own little fantasy world with "Disney gone awry" styled characters as his playmates, making cartoony sound effects to describe his experiences. He creates the images that shape our urban world, from the dark commentaries in his fine art paintings and drawings to the cute little aliens sucking up the Earth in his board graphics. And somewhere in between those polar extremes are the innovative graphic design, clothing, poster, and unique advertising campaigns that he creates for his own skateboard company Rhythm. Having grown up in the madness of Miami, this Cuban American artist had his first public appearances in the form of expressive graffiti in his hometown crew Free Agents Miami. I met him on a skateboard demo trip I had to Florida, where I was hanging out with Felix. I think Jose was about 15 then, and I saw some of his amazing drawings and asked him if he'd do a graphic for New Deal. We were drawing graphics out and doing hand seperations back then, and he did some great artwork. Today he is the most influential artist in skateboarding, and one of the most creative artists around. In his young career as an internationally known artist. If you've ever ridden a skateboard you have already seen so much of his artwork anywhere in the world for the last 6-7 years, and if you didn't realize that they was his creations you were enjoying, guess what: Now You Do. -Andy Howell

With deep roots in american underground and hip-hop culture, HAZE manages to capture and represent the essence of "urban style" without being restricted or typecast by it. Where Eric Haze was a major contributor to the golden age of graffiti coming into it's own as an art form, and the accomplishment of hip-hop graphics making their mark on a global level, his company has also been at the forefront of the underground streetwear movement as it grew to achieve mainstream recognition and visibility. Presenting styles that range in influence from skate culture, pop art, hot rodding, and industrialism - while still also being true to his roots as a graffiti artist - HAZE has proven that his unique brand of ecclecticism consistently captures the pulse of contemporary culture, dealing in universal themes and iconography while still maintaining his own signature styles as a designer. Now, while the market and face of streetwear has changed radically

over the last few years with major corporations like Tommy Hilfiger and Polo taking their cues from streetwear and co-opting it's styles, HAZE has maintained it's posture and integrity as a true independant, consistent in their approach to their original identity, raising the level of their product and image without reaching out for corporate sponsorship or subscribing to more mainstream marketing tactics. HAZE has also maintained it's commitment to pushing the boundries of what their company represents by developing other products outside just the clothing line, producing graphics driven furniture, jewelry, accessories, and skateboards over the past 3 years. In addition, Eric Haze has maintained his status and involvement as a designer for outside projects, including the recent design of a new logo for Quincy Jones's record label "QWEST", participating in a number of design exhibitons around the world, and presenting his own underground hip-

hop record compilation " New York Reality Check 101" with DJ Premier on London Records. Eric Haze regards his philosophy and approach to clothing as consistent with his history as an artist over the previous two decades, as much a question of impact as it is of product:
"Twenty years ago the mission as a graffiti artist was to get our message across to the largest audience possible, using the trains as the means of exposure and distribution, and integrating our art into the fabric and consciousness of peoples everyday lives. The clothing now serves the same purpose in many ways - allowing me a similar kind of artistic freedom, with the ability to reach an even larger audience on a global scale. Even though the level and integrity of the product I put out is my main focus as an artist, it is the sense of participating in the evolution of our cultures that makes it really inspiring and worthwhile."

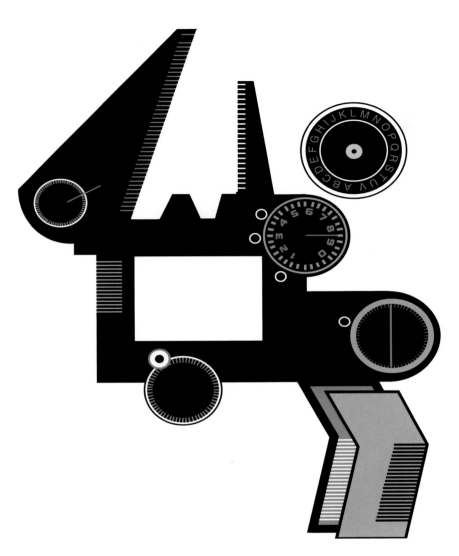

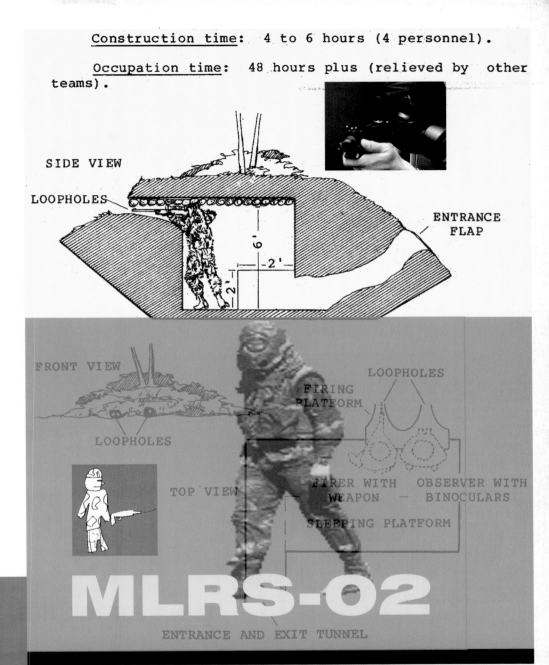

SIDE VIEW

LOOPHOLES

ENTRANCE FLAP

6'

2'

2'

2'

FRONT VIEW

LOOPHOLES

FIRING PLATFORM

LOOPHOLES

LOOPHOLES

TOP VIEW

FIRER WITH WEAPON

OBSERVER WITH BINOCULARS

SLEEPING PLATFORM

MLRS-02

ENTRANCE AND EXIT TUNNEL

Figure 4-11. Semipermanent hide position.

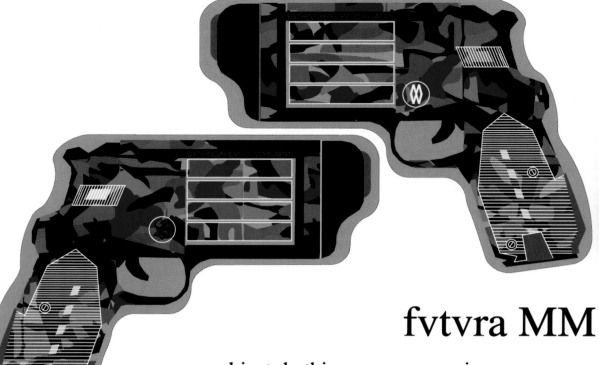

FL
FUTURA LABORATORIES

fvtvra MM

subject: bathingapevsmowaxjapan
futuraoptics
the better to see you with

Over the last decades **Futura** became definitely one of the most influential artists of New York's graffiti scene. In the late-seventies you found him trespassing the yards of the Metropolitan Transportation Authorithies bombing trains and walls. Just a few years later authentic and dynamic art got him into holier-than-thou galleries, where he, besides his fellow graffiti artists Basquiat and Kenny Schaaf, gained recognition as a pure street artist. Nevertheless, Futura's creativity didn't rest in exhibition or subways. He challenges contemporary forms of expression. He took his skills to everyday art, like designing casual garmets for the legendary street wear-brands 'GFS' and 'Project Dragon' or creating brilliant artworks for London based record label Mo'Wax. His recent, presumably never ending output includes producing robot toys for the Japanese kindergardens.

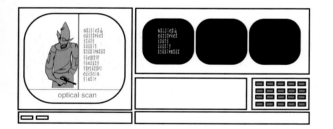

optical scan

tarantula execution team

Jose Gomez. advertdesign for his own company Rythm

flag by erik brunetti

No Skateboarding
=FUCK YOU= VK HATE
SDMC 84.12

For Safety's Sake

Beer City™
SKATEBOARDS
MILWAUKEE, WI U.S.A.

PEDESTRIAN

WANTED BY FB

FRED REBELL

the empire strikes back

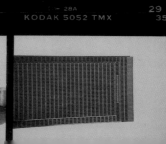

KODAK 5052 TMX

joe sbegner- s.f. b.s. 5-0 f.s. 180 off

airto jackson- a day at pier no: 7 in san francisco   airto jackson- s.f. b.s. tailslide

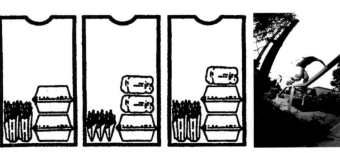

Adrian Lopez backside tailslides near the
U.C.S.D. in San Diego. so what's in his lunchbag

ronnie creager- switchstance hardflipping down a flight of stairs in santa ana, ca. ronnie is a true muscle car enthusiastic

lavar mcbride- nosebluntslide across a block at the world's famous pier no: 7 in san fran.

clockwise photospecification: **matt mumford** b.s. 50-50 on a dark scary rail. **socal buddy** s/s 180 heelflip over a fire-hydrant.
steve olson lipslide down a rail, while his fellows take care of the street sweepers. **brian patch** f.s. ollie at chicken's pool.
mark 'the gonz' gonzales the oldschool is new newschool. carjump.

below: surpreme video installation

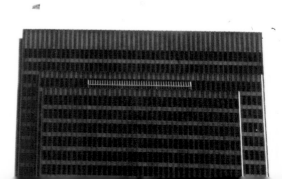

we like to thank poolconstructionworkers. especially those in california, cause they lay the foundation that took skateboarding to another level. **brian patch** and his buddy doesn't care about it anyway! a regular pool session at chickens pool, huntington ca. illustration by **andy howell**

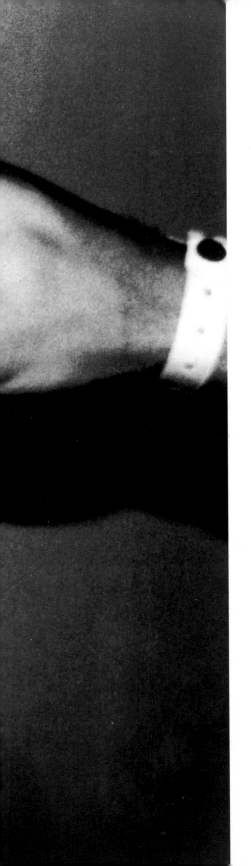

the most
sought-after
stuntman

skateboarding in

chad muska. he has still a long way to go on this california rail. 50-50 with dr. octagon voice in the background.

a 38 feet tall roll in, **danny way** had checked the wind direction before breaking the world's record highest air. part of the world's la. advert campaign on the skateshoe sector. **foto by ballard** for **dc shoe co.**

New York City Represent

Monitored by the
Metro-North Police

opposite page: from top to bottom nyc represent! **vinnie ponte** brooklyn bank ollie bomb. **rodney torres** heelflip shovit.
danny supa nosegrind. recon the **zooyork** assasination squad!
this page: **the brooklyn banks**, nyc's favorite skatespot, at night by elyashkevich.

ZOO YORK

MIXTAPES

c.w.:vinnie ponte, rob gangemini, the zooyork crew, quim cardona.
all photos by elyashkevich & campbell

l.l. & run dmc, back in the daze. leaders of the golden age, around eightiefive.
© glen e. friedman

...ry is rough, my neighborhood is
tough...but I still sport gold and I'm out to
crush... My name is Cool J, I devastate the
show but I couldn't survive without my
...radio... Terrorizing the neighbors with a heavy bass, I keep suckers...
...by the look on my face... My radio's bad from the boulevard...m
a...hop gangster and my name is Todd..."—from *I Can't Live*
Without My Radio–L.L. Cool J

MOS DEF

6astard

"A...B-BOYS ROC
THE WORLD..."
- THE UNIVERSAL MAGNETI

© jackel

independent as fuck, company flow.
©eddie otchere

Hatred, jealousy, envy, anger, despair, animosity and deceit personify the ultimate evil for Kendrick Davis. They threaten America's future, he's convinced, the youth, the hip-hop generation, Generation Z, whatever you want to call them. But in the days of Moet sipping, Lexus cruising and mobile swinging Mack Daddies, fed by a dangerous diet of name brand apparel, artillery and narcotics, Kendrick Davis aka Jeru The Damaja had enough. It was 1993 and the Brooklyn born rapper took up the mic and with it the responsibility and duty to redirect hip hop's lost souls and smack the flesh off gangsta poseurs like the blood out of a good Argentinian steak . "The main purpose of my records is to make dope records," Jeru explains. "But the purpose of the music that's on this record is to provoke thought. That's all my music is here to do: provoke thought. By provoking thought, I switch and change the order of things."

"The Sun Rises In the East" and "Wrath Of The Math" were the first two mindblowing, thought-provoking longplayers the hip hop prophet has released to date. On both masterpieces Jeru's unique stakkato-like raps were melted with the fresh beats of the most respected and loved beat constructor and flow conductor in the hip hop genre: DJ Premier. "We have a chemistry that a lot of the artists and producers don't have. He gives me the beat and bang, I write the rhyme to fit the beat," Jeru sighs. "It's like one creation, something that flows together naturally 'cos in this world everything is mathematics, and now is the time when mathematics is coming forcefully. I am personified mathematics and as such I bring the rage in the form of powerful and unpredictable hurricanes and tornados."

Wherever the fake playaz and fake gangstas
are, I'm coming to see you - east or west.
Cos you are those individuals
fucking shit up in hip hop

In his rhymes Jeru tackles pretty much everything that bothers, or at least should bother the hip hop world just before the millenium: institutionalized racism, mis-education, covert government actions and the East coast West coast saga. But Jeru doesn't just diss blatantly, nah, he introduces a level of wordplay, cheekieness and science into the artform that left most headz quiet in awe. Just check tracks like "You Can't Stop The Prophet", "Da Bichez", "One Day" or "Ya Playin' Yaself" and you know what I'm sayin. This man is dope to the max and despite being as tall as an average parking meter he's got the mental, but also the physical stamina. As for the future, shit's gonna happen faster than you can look. Expect a new Jeru album very soon, soundtrack appearances - his music featured amongst others in 'Clockers' and 'Pump Ya Fist' and hopefully some European ads for this dope little fruit juice 'Squeez'r' which he promotes in the States. Until then, keep it all tight and listen to the 'Ru: "Wherever the fake playaz and gangstas are, I'm coming to see you - east or west. 'Cos you are those individuals fucking shit up in hip hop."

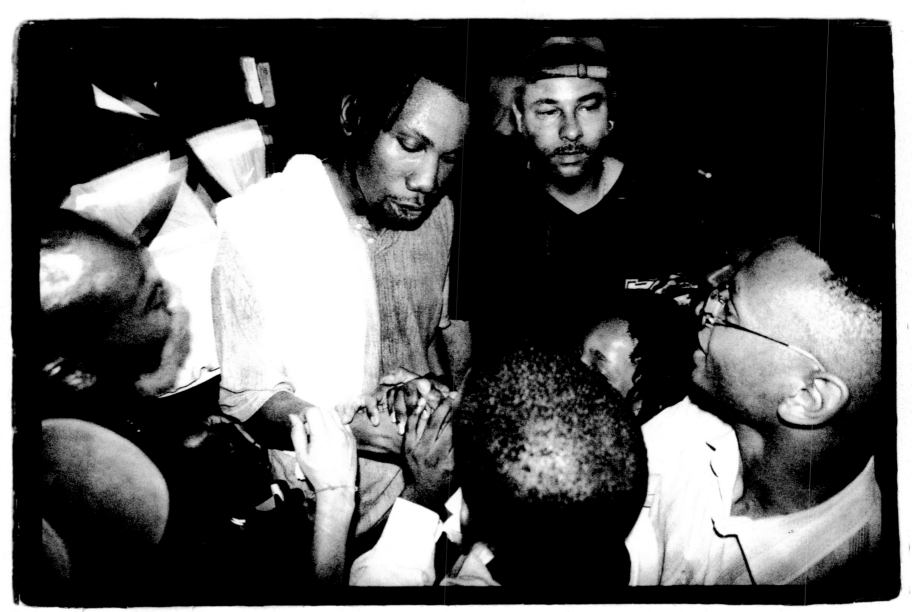

krs one, the teacher, the preacher now? ©eddie otchere

Digable Planets walk through New York City like they were born to do just that. While most of mid-morning Manhattan strides purposefully, the warm fall day barely registering, the three Planets sort of glide along, taking in as much of the city as they can. As I walk with Butterfly, Doodlebug and Ladybug from EMI's midtown offices to Central Park, they seem particularly determined not to miss a thing. They check out a man sitting on the street selling arty-looking black-and-white posters, then pause for a moment to listen to a street-corner saxophonist. And why not? "New York is a museum," Butterfly rapped on "Pacifics," and the Planets, all Brooklyn residents, appear to be its patrons. They're just cool like that.

We walk to the small lake at the southern end of the park. It's surrounded by benches, occupied mostly by businessmen taking early outdoor lunches. "This is a hideaway," Butterfly says, all of a sudden, glancing around him. "It's like where the Establishment comes to get away from the wickedness they've caused."

Whoah. Pretty cynical for a guy who at first glance seems so laid back, but there's more to Butterfly than meets the eye. He's mellow—but he's also dedicated and focused, and his calm, hipster cool masks a quiet intensity. He's the kind of guy who would take an innocent-sounding insect name to express a Marxist concept of communal action; the kind of guy who raps about kicking back with jazz records on a slow Sunday morning but says he's really too busy to enjoy such leisure himself.

Call him Ishmael. His real name is Ishmael Butler. And call Ladybug "Mecca" and Doodlebug "Knowledge." Though their real names are Mary Ann Vieira and C. Irving, those are the monikers they go by, the insect plumes reserved for Digable Planets.

In a way, those insect names, so good at promising a sort of intergalactic hip hop, describe the part of the Planets as their funky, jazzy hip-hop.

a true hip hop activist, at least a true black moviemaker ©eddie otchere

SPIKE LEE

A STATEMENT OF TURNTABLE SCIENCE HIPHOPS AVANTGARDE IS ON THE RISE

In 1982, major record companies first expressed interest in signing rap's founding fathers. It was a time when majors like Elektra and Columbia first made apparent their interest in the new urban form of dance music by distributing independent labels like the seminal Def Jam imprint and by putting up money for individual artists such as the Sugar Hill Gang and Grandmaster Flash.

Hip Hop seemed to be on the track to great success representing a new youth culture that was thriving in urban areas throughout the country and was ready to be accepted by middleclass America. But soon enough the novelty wore off for the frickle record companies and they moved on to a more profitable pop genre.

This was ar ound 1985 when cutting edge independents began to pick-up the corporate stack. It was already the beginning of the middle ages for hip-hop when small labels like Tommy Boy, Profile, and Next Plateau took control of the market and laid the framework for the genre to grow both creatively, fostering the artistic development of such artists as Run DMC, LL Cool J, Kurtis Blow, EPMD, and Mantronix, and for transcending them into the mass market. According to Bobbito The Barber, owner of indie Fondle´em Records in New York, "the world whole period between ´86 and ´89 was a great age for (hip-hop) music because all of the indies were controlling the market." But with all of this success the majors again wanted a piece - rather most - of the pie. It was not until 1989 when the money-making business again became involved, as they realized the investment opportunity in this relatively uncharted consumer territory. No longer was rap music being put out by those who created it and cared about its artistic well-being. But big record companies and now television like MTV started to wave dollar bills, attracting the interest of the majority of the industry´s talent, signing dozens of the new artists, and taking over the distribution or buying up many indie - labels. As a result not only did smaller labels suffer, so did the original format of the music´s original medium - the radio. "That was a dark period for rap music. It was the beginning of a time when radio air play almost ceased and videos were becoming popular. As a result records weren´t being sold on the basis of artistic merit but rather on its imaging and video marketability."

This is the current state of hip-hop: fueled by big money, expensive cars, and champagne swilling mack-daddies - as viewed on television and album covers, it is the classic case example of what is to be nouveau riche. Making too much money too fast has convoluted its very existence, watering down its content and stunting its artistic growth. But as the corporate ideal moves in one direction there is an underground movement that is trying to salvage it from its exploitative clutches and is attempting to bring it back. This is what Kevin Harewood, General Manager of Los Angeles' indie-label Correct Records, calls "the pendulum effect." He describes the underground scene as "getting stronger because of all the negative feeling about majors."

Represented by a new school of artists and record labels, increased radio air-play on increasingly poplar DJ mix shows, and blostering support from its jaded audience the independent movement in America could be hip hop´s saving grace.

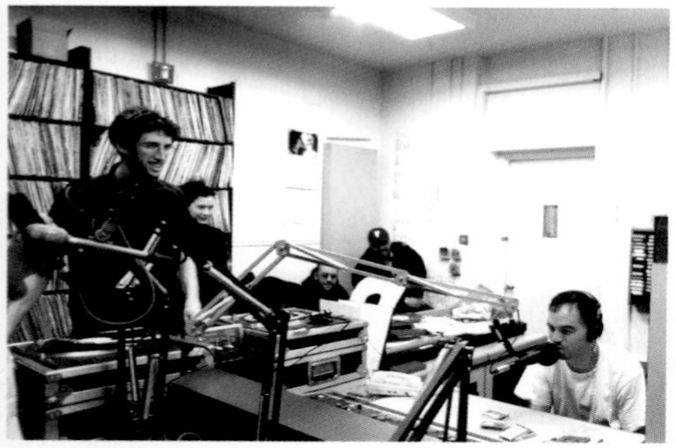

STRETCH ARMSTRONG dj'ing, **BOBITO THE BARBER** mc'ing

The most fundamental problem in major hip-hop is not the artists' lack of vision but it is the limitations set forth by its distributors. It is the label who signs musicans as products to be sold and, therefore, they have to market their artists' assets to the general public. Ultimately, it is the label that must gain attention for their products so they must illustrate their talents - if they have some or not - any way they can. Whether it is an artist´s unique style, musicanship, fashion, or appearance one or few of these elements must be made apparent to its audience via promotions. Since the dawn of the music video the priority of these elements has been redefined. Now the most effective and obvious manner in which to sell a musical product is through superfical appearance. The simplest marketing techniques are used: Do a survey of your target audience, find out their most attractive interest, project these ideas of desirability in the media, and wham: you have a music video or an album cover - a misogynist driving a Lexus, talking on a cell-phone, drinking Moet et Chandon, and smoking mad weed! Yeah, livin´ large goes a long way in the media, and their focus on a phony exterior has destroyed rap´s integrity.

Indie-labels have recognized their need, modeling itself after the "golden age" of rap during the mid to late eighties, indie-labels are popping up everywhere.

With a D.I.Y. attitude like Fondie´em, Dolo, Searchlight, and Official are representing the East; and labels like Soulsides, Invisibl Scratch Piklz Recordings, Kingsize, and Correct are standing strong in the West, Don´t misunderstand though they still want to sell records–just without all of the pretense. They have a different marketing approach; they focus on the musical talent of the artist.

Maybe these labels aren´t generating as much attention as the majors, because aside from their different sales approach they lack of funds for up-scale advertising, but at least they are giving control back to artists. They are encouraging artists to experiment and broaden the scope of the genre. They want them to focus on their music and draw its audience through talent. "We work with the artists and try to set up a deal where we say, do something different. We can´t offer a lot of money up front but maybe after good sales we can offer higher loyalties. Our artists are really important to us; we´re working for the artists," says Nick Eisenman of New York´s Dolo Recors (which he co-runs with DJ Stretch Armstrong).

As a result recent rap acts like Non-Phixtion, Company Flow, Dutchmin, and the Soulsides crew are able to expand the spectrum of the music. They are a new school - exploring new territories, using different sampling and vocal techniques, writing more accessible and more creative lyrics, and in the process bringing the artistry back to art; thus, taking the music from out of its rest - to the next level. The indie market isn´t just for underground acts either. The doctor of futuristic beats - Kool Keith, Greg Nice, and the king himself, Afrika Bambaataa, are all doing independent projects. They are attracted to the smaller scale companies to free the harness of corporate control. Rappers like Kool Keith have taken money earned from major deals and applied it to producing more underground tracks free of artistic sponsorship. "In the last couple of years a lot of people are getting sick of being jerked - both financially and creatively - by majors," says Bobbito The Barber. "They´re being pushed to sell as many records as possible; they´re being pressured to produce hits."

It´s not just more control over the product that these acts are pursuing either. It´s also a larger percentage of proceeds from their recordings, more control over contractual agreements, and a more personal relationship with the label. Many times smaller labels will work with artists with little more than a handshake and even split off percentage from sales. Owners like Bobbito will only work with musicians that he trusts and doesn´t deal with contracts. He also splits 50/50 of an artist´s profits. "That´s a pretty large royality for someone like The Arsonist who has sold over 4.000 records in New York alone, he insists." And these kinds of informal agreements create a greater loyality between the two sides.

There is more personal relationship with the artist and a small label because they are more collaborative. It takes both parties´ efforts to see a release sell. This personal relationship causes the label to care more than just about their own pay-checks. Nick Eisenman says, "We´re working with artists and I take it as a personal challenge to help them sell their records. We even sometimes personally drive to record stores and hand distribute material. "This attitude crosses over into the industry as well. Different labels sometimes work collaboratively to promote hip-hop as a whole. The existence of an underground scene creates a greater sense of solidarity among all of its members - even among different labels. Dolo records, for instance, is soon to release an independent rap sampler. It will feature material from over twenty different labels. The idea, says Nick, is to "create a definitive collection" and to "expose indie-artists to a more mainstream audience. "Everyone who participates on the compilation will benefit from the exposure - particulary the artists. The collection is also an example of the non-existence of barries between different scenes within hip-hop.

Also particular to the world of indie-hip-hop is the absence of envy among artists and different posses. There is no media-generated hype like the supposed East coast/West coast war or rival gang-related name-calling. Q-Bert (also known for his work with the mad Doctor Octagon) of the Invisibl Sratch Piklz denounces it as "Pretty much for the ignorant - t shouldn´t matter if it´s east or west coast; it should be about whether it´s whack or fresh. We ain´t trippin off that concept at all." Kevin Harewood agrees with the turntable wizard. His L.A.-based Correct label "signs acts from all over the U.S." For exsample, one of their most successful artists Black Attack is from New York yet they are based on the West coast. And what about native New Yorker Kool Keith who now lives in on the West coast as well. To quote Q-Bert´s latest Piklz partner, DJ Yoga-Frog: "We don´t think about that bullshit, we're just all about scratching."

Independent labels and artists are not alone in their underground attack against the establishment. Radio stations are taking these acts to the airwaves, giving much needed play to independent artists on ever-becoming-more-popular DJ mix shows. They are and promoting music for its own sake-free of stylized imagery.

Radio shows the like the Stretch Armstrong and Bobbito Show, on HOT 97 as well as Columbia University´s WKCL, and the DJ Rags (owner of San Diego-based Kingsize Records) Show, on the Tiujuana - based Z-90, play an integral role in the genre of expanding its reaches creatively while redefining its identity to one closer to the so called "golden age". A time when small radio stations during the late seventies and early eighties were the only other medium than on record where one could hear fresh new sounds from the street.

These radio shows, in parallel to the indie-label movement, are newly established - dating back at most only five or six years. The Stretch and Bobbito Show on WKCL is an institution. Already in the sixth year its success on collage radio lead to another weekly show on New York´s most popular hip-hop station. Twice a week the two spin an all underground set, primarily focusing only on exposing indie-artists.

Similary DJ Rags´show (every Saturday night) on Z-90, a station owned by his brother, has aired for three and a half years. It´s broadcast from Tiujuana, Mexico, yet its signal is so strong that it reaches all over Southern California. It features mainly local San Diego acts and he does remixes of his own and showcases them on the show. "When we started, you could tell people were asking to be educated in rap," says Rags. Now, several years later it seems his job is half-way complete. Independent hip-hop in America is making its mark. By adopting a "golden age" old school attitude labels, artists, and DJs are changing the manner in which we perceive the genre. No longer embracing the media -hyped "Big Willie" mentality they are leaving all of pretense behind and exchange it for innovation and locally to the scene. Maybe major record companies could learn a few things, and then new hip-hop would really have a chance. by dan shumate

Q-BERT & **YOGA FROG** mad skills for the turntablelists

WORD SOUND

masters of nothing.
the philosophy of subterrain hiphop conspiracy.

PEACE TO MY QUEEN EQUALITY, MY SEEDS, MY OLD EARTH, AND MY FAMILY. PEACE TO THE GODS & EARTHS, THE WU-FAMILY MEMBERS AND ALL THOSE WHO SUPPORT THE RZA'. PEACE TO DIVINE FOR DOING WHAT HE DO. PROPER EQUALITY CAPTIVATES 'CONTROLLED EMOTIONS!

...TO MY MOM & DAD, MY WU-FAMI- ... MY BLACK WOMAN & ... SEEDS, AND ALL ... ... PEACE TO THE

...LAW LIBRARIES: IT'S TIME TO FUCK THESE DEVILS' AT THEIR OWN TRICKS AND TRADES - WE DOCTORS, LAWYERS, ELECTRICIANS' CREATING DEVELOPMENTS WITHIN OUR COMMUNITY. PEACE TO ALL MY OUTTA STATE MAJOR NIGGAZ!!! YOU KNOW WHO YALL ARE. PEACE TO ALL THE FANS WHO CAME THRU AND SHOWED US LOVE FROM DAY ONE...LOVE YA NIGGAZ!!! AND TO ALL MY ELROPEAN & INTERNATIONAL SPOKES PEOPLE..... LOVE YALL. I'MA SEE YALL NIGGAZ WHEN I'M ON TOUR. LAST BUT NOT LEAST... FUCK ALL YALL FAKE PROPRIETORS. YALL CAN'T FUCK WITH OUR HUSTLE CAUSE WE GET STRONGER EVERY TIME YALL GO AGAINST US AND TO ALL YALL FAGGOT ASS RADIO NIGGAZ THAT DON'T BE SUPPORTING OUR SHIT. DON'T EVER SPEAK TO ME CAUSE I'M LIABLE TO SPIT IN YA FUCKING FACE. PEACE TO MY MOM, NANA, PEACE TO MY LADY AND MY FAMILY WHICH CONSISTS OF HALF THE WORLD....I LOVE YALL!!!!!! YEAH, AND ALL THE CATS W/ BANGING SYSTEMS, WARNING! PLAY THIS SHIT LOUD AS FUCK!!!

GRANDMA RUBY, PRINCE, AND THE WHOLE GRANT FAMILY. ...PSON FAMILY, CAPPADONNA, STREET, CARLTON FISK, POOH, RECCO, KAY, ...EK, DENNIS, SHYHEIM, BLUE RASPBER- ...A, KILLARMY, SUNZ OF MAN, ROYAL DISCIPLE, LA THE DARK MAN, DADDY- GRAVE DIGGAZ, FORCE MD'S, 12 ...ROYAL, B-LOVER, FLUTE, HOPE, KIN- ...IC ATTITUDE, SHORTY CESS, CHIANNA, ...B. & SLICK (WITH HER STINKIN' ASS), ...GGAS, POPPA RON, TIM DOG, RADER ...ANK FROM TENNESSEE, OUR PEOPLES ...OWN, SHEISTE (GET THAT ED-U-MA- ...OMANI (GET THAT DOCTOR'S DEGREE) ...RATULATIONS TO AL OLGGIE ON HIS ...MUCH LOVE TO GIANNA, MICHELLE, ...DIE, & MS. ENITH, WE LOVE YOU ALL. ...EEPS WE FORGOT TO MENTION, AND TO ...IRLS WE'VE LOVED BEFORE, HAHA, HAHA. ...I, (STINKIN' ASSES), OUR 'LOUD' ...ES, DAWN-MARIE GRAY, AND ALL ...E 'NBA' NIGGAZ! LASTLY, PEACE TO ...CHRIS (HANDLE THAT RADIO). ...HARLENE, RETAIL, VIDEO & PRESS OUT- ...KS TO ALL PUBLICATIONS WHO GIVE ...D ALL OF OUR RHYME PEERS, VOCAL- ...ICIANS, THAT SUPPORT WU-TANG! ...E TO EVERYBODY IN THE MUSIC & TELE- ...WORKS. PEACE TO TYCIANNA ON HER ...JACKIE LAPARDO (KEEP YOUR HEAD ...T YOUR BACK DON'T FORGET ABOUT ...ADATION). MUCH RESPECTS TO THE ...F THE LATE RAPPERS, REST IN PEACE. ...E OF THE WORLD MAKE SURE YOU GET ...CIAL. OFFICIAL. OFFICIAL!!!!!!

PEACE TO MY OLD EARTH, MY SEEDS, THE WU-FAMILY, MAN, WOMAN, AND CHILD. EAST & WEST COAST NEED TO STOP THAT BULLSHIT CAUSE THERE'S ONLY ONE COAST AND THAT'S THE EARTH! MUTHA FUCKERS!

SNAP OUT THAT BULLSHIT, THAT SHIT STARTED OVER HERE!

FUCK A SHOUT OUT PEACE TO MY MOMS, MY SON DONTE, GRAND- MA, GRANDPA, UNCLE JASON, MATTHEW BOO, BLACK, BLIZ, RADE. ... SHAY, OOO, CHOICE, KILLA ... RULER SIN, BORN, NINTH PRINCE, SHOGUN, DON PACINO, SUPREME, SUNZ OF-MAN-HELL RAIZER, PRODIGAL, KILLAH PRIEST. 60 SECOND, SHYHEIM, TEKITHA, CANDY, ROYAL FAM, NAS, DEF SQUAD, PARK HILL PROJECTS. NEW BRIGHTEN, SHAOLIN, SCHOTT FREE & HAR- BOR KREW, DIVINE, POWER, THE WU-STAFF: TANYA, JILL, SHERIN, VINCE, MERV, CHARLENE & LOUD, WU-WEAR: ALFARO, CYNAMIN, CLEVE, MIKE, KAT, PAPA WU, RANCE, LIL FREE, MOOK, ALL THE GODS & EARTHS, ATLANTA, LOS ANGE- LES, FLORIDA, CHI-TOWN, AND NIGGAZ ALL OVER!

PEACE TO MY OLD EARTH, MY FAMI- LY, ALL THE GODS & EARTHS, ALL MY BLACK PEOPLE, PUER- TO RICANS, LATI NOS, ALL MY NIGGAZ, STA- PLETON, PARK HILL ...

WU-WEAR: CLEVE, MIKE, ALFARO, LOUNGER, CYNAMIN, KAT, JALLELA, SHARON. DESIGNERS: ...NEY, RAY AND STAFF. WU-WEAR (ATLANTA): TARIF, JIHAD, COOKIE, ERIK, JENNIFER, MARY ...WU-WEAR (VIRGINIA): TIM, RANCE, LIL FREE, AND STAFF. WU-WEAR (CALIFORNIA).

PEACE TO MEDI- NA: BED-STUY, EAST NEW YORK, FLAT- BUSH, BROWNSVILLE, MAN, WOMAN, CHILD, ALL THE GODS & THE EARTHS, MY WHOLE FAMILY FROM NEW YORK TO SUMTER, SOUTH CAROLINA.

ALL MAN, WOMAN, AND CHILD THAT SUPPORT WU-TANG, OUR EXECUTIVES - DIVINE AND OUR D.J. - MATHEMATICS, PEACE TO THE LOUD STAFF. WU-STAFF: SOPHIA, KIN... SHER- INE, MOOK, JILL, VINCE, MERV, PAPA...

Meth on the album "Wu Tang Forever":

"It's 25 tracks strong. Look how many people we had. We had so much talent, two platinum and five gold records. All that talent on one album had to be a double CD. U-God, Master Killah, Inspektah Deck, Capadonna und Street get more exposure this time around. It's about the facts of life, you know, about god and devil, facts about the New World Order, the millenium, just facts of life. There is no comparison whatsoever with `36 Chambers' ` cos we are older and wiser and the music reflects that, you know. It moved up, but it is always through the heart though, no doubt. Everybody is using clischees such as `keep it real', `represent' and all that. It's just getting to the point where you get tired of hearing that shit ` cos nobody is keeping it real and nobody is representing. That's why we had to make a statement. Bottom line."

Meth on the "5 Per Cent Nation Of Islam" and their `Living Mathematics', the philosophical/religious background of the Wu Tang Clan:

"Everything is dealt with through mathematics, sort of a numeric system. Everything from here to the universe out there. And we deal with planets. We don't mean as far as Pluto and Uranus and all that shit, we mean the mind as a planet. If you break the syllables down in `planet', it's "plan it" and whether you plan it out in your mind and deal with things through the mental first. Through knowledge, wisdom and understanding. Or take the word `knowledge', for example. It means `to know the ledge'. Know the ledge, so you won't fall off the edge. Into the devil civilisation. That's our way of life, our culture. So each word that I use, I manifest. I live it out, each and every day. I have to."

Meth on changes in his personal life as the biggest Wu Tang star with 1,1 million sold copies of his solo album and an US No.1 with the Mary J.Blige joint:

"Acting, I am getting caught for a lot more things now. I am distancing myself more from the paparazzi. I hate them fuckers. For me it's like I am one of those people, if I can't see it, I can't trust it. And half those parties, on these talkshows where they bring all these stars out, they just piss me off. They have no personalities. It turns your stomach when you actually sit amongst those and you are part of it. I am distancing myself away from that. That's not even my style boy. When everywhere you go people are telling you how dope you is and how good you look and all this, after a while you start believing it and you don't work as hard. You ain't got to kiss my ass dude, I know what I am doing."

Meth on Tupac and Biggie:

"I don't know, I am (rolls his eyes, looking slightly crazy) buh, shit. I am not into that at all (long silence). It's bad. Just `cos I am a rapper, it doesn't mean I am into shit like this. No Fuck that. They can freak out. I mean, I have seen shit like that happen in my whole childhood man. It ain't nothing new, but it's just very bad. Bottom line. But I am neither representing Biggie or Tupac."

Ol' Dirty on Tupac and Biggie:

"If I said on stage that it was the CIA that killed them, that's what I mean. Off course they (Biggie and Tupac!) already told me. I know it was the CIA, there is no doubt about it. It's common sense. But they are not bad anymore. It's good now. There are with me know.Okay. So they are fine."

Meth on `dissing' the fake Hip Hop pimps and players:

"I don't give nobody no false fame of my shit, I never say no nigger name on my shit. Hell not! I see him in a club and whoop his ass before I do that. Word! If someone did piss me off, I wouldn't tell `cos the element of surprise is so good. It's like if a person knows that you don't like him, they are expecting something. Nah man, I keep it here and here (head & heart). But I don't even have feelings to hate shit. If I hate something, I kill it. So I don't hate at all."

Meth on the Crack-CIA debate:

"They put it in there with the intent of us, using it and then killing ourselves off. That's why it was so easy and cheap to get. There was a point when all the kids went into dealing. I mean you make 500 dollars on half a day. Fast, tax free. But then it got to the point where people started coming from the suburbs, it started affecting these so called real families, these after school special families and shit like that. Like little Timmy has a drug problem now, you know that type of shit. And when that kind of shit was happening, (looks very dark and changes voice), then it became a real big problem. The government has never adressed it. Let's put it that way. They have never actually said we didn't do it. Oh man, George Bush was the biggest drug dealer, him and Reagan. Word up man."

Meth on racist New York cops in his hood Parkhill aka Killer Hills, Staten Island:

"I have been experiencing that since day one when I was a shorty walking around my block, harassing brothers older than me. But they were looking at me too, you know like "when you get older you gonna be one of mine". Know what I mean. Meaning that they are waiting for you to get to a certain age to lock your ass up too and start harrassing you. It's all one cycle and they got us trapped in an area, where there is no hope. Killer Hills, Parkhill. That got that name `cos a lot of bodies used to show up there, dead bodies and shit."

Meth on his filmplans:

"Yes, I've done some stuff and I get quite a few scripts sent. The biggest thing was "Copland" with Sly Stallone, Robert de Niro, Harvey Keitel, It's a film about this fucked up cop community. They are all living in the same kind of area shit and the question is : Who is policing the cops? It was fun, you know but it's not worth the show money. That shit is garbage. When you see what Demy Moore gets. $10 Million a movie, she signs a contract and gets 40 million and does 4 movies. Oh man, that's the kind of contract I want. I would strip. You know what a record contract looks like - ouhh that's bad shit compared. I would stoke it up like Sly Stallone, no problem.."

Meth on promo tours, `out of state hoes' and music in general:

"I don't really dig the shows, the promos, the out of state hoes, non

And finally...Meth on the hottest and spiciest Spice Girl around:

"Ey yo Mel B. Spice girls. This is Meth my girl. Word up, I will blow your back off the map. Blow your back off the map. Pow. Bang, bang, bang, bang. Fast . Haha. Love me!"

word: goetz w

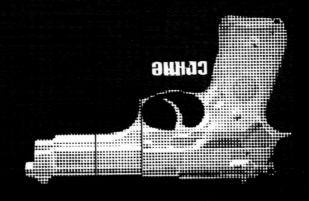

Why. Trip Hop sucks in 96' <

dj shadow, u.n.k.l.e. member, chillin' at the old
mowax rooftop residence in london 96,
90 degrees in the shade.

ENDTRODUCING......

dj krush lodown in 97

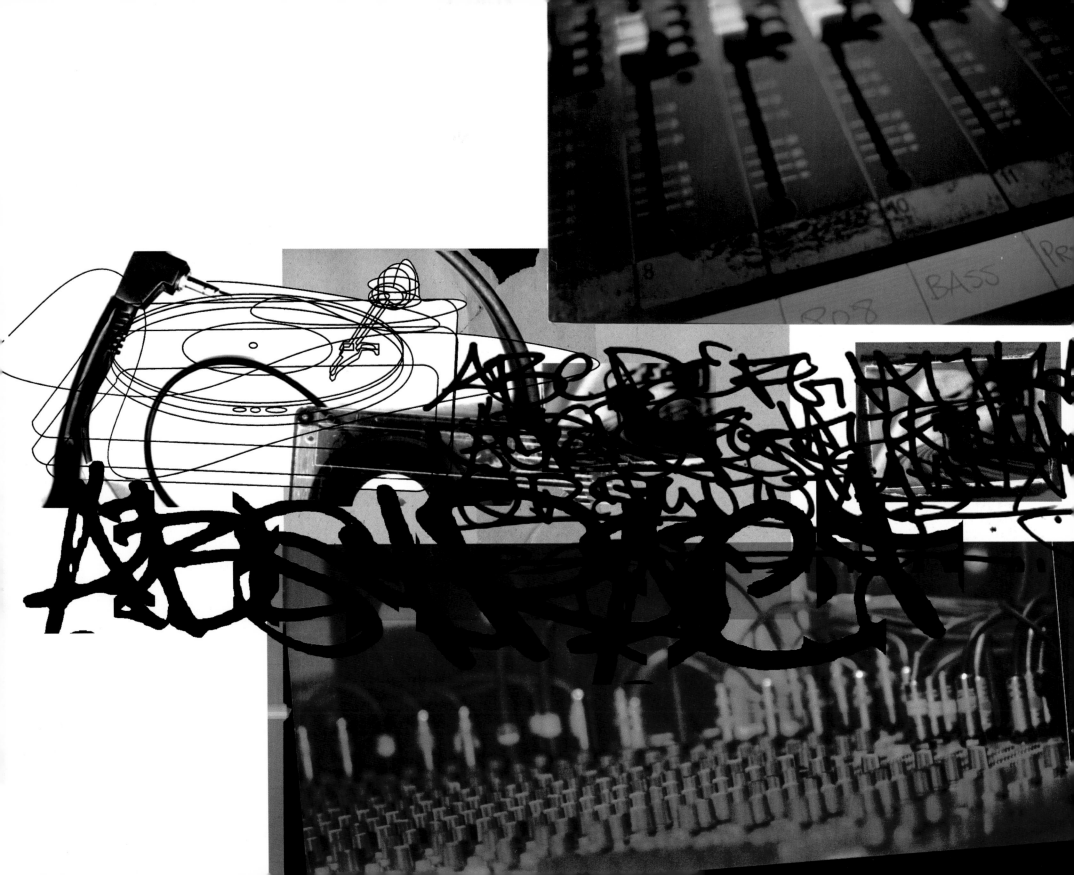

#286 the end of abstract turn-abstraction mission complete

more abstract turntablelism, small b-boy eve, outcast's elevator, massive attack

massive

Three...the magical meeting of digits... always the uneven companion within the balance of the force.
The 3rd optic is needed to oversee, overstand & inquire, without their sum parts the triangle named Attica Blues would be incomplete.
For this group of African Londonites Africa is in 3 places – Ghana, Nigeria, Egypt.

The third eye watches over the second and the first. It's a mindstate that evolves around 80-125 bpm, divided by three...it's simple mathematics. One third of the membership, Charlie Williams, speaks and acts out the closest image of the human, as polyrhythm, from a stone-slurred accoustic chill-out to a frenzied technoid bugout...hip hop and everything inbetween. He recalls: "When we first started we couldn't get an SP 1200 in England and there was only a handful of bands doing it,
Massive Attack and Smith and Mighty, being just two. Noone hadn't even heard of Portishead.
Now it's saturation.
It's so easy to get equipment right now and loop a beat up, and that's it.
Now everyone and their mum has got suicide vocals on hip hop records,
I'm bored of it and so is the listener."

The second eye suddenly blinks open in agreement. Tony drops in: "The industry dictates what happens. If you are not favourite by the industry, then you have no place, no matter how good your music is."
Tony Nwachuku is the ultimate enigma. A labyrinth of musical ideas, black politics and new age beatsavant. He walks it as he talks it, as he plays it. If "Hal" was a homosapien Tony would be Akai recreating the SP 1200, sheer genius like Guiness at times, bitter at other intervals.

The everchanging third, second or first eye Roba El-Essawy can be an absolute mystery with a personality which contains a mixture between South London's smokiest vibes and innerchild songstress. b-girl tomboyishness it's a contradiction, even more unnerving in her musical persona. The face of a beautiful heavenly cherub and then the voice...a piercing torch song feel like walking on the sands of the Middle East, barefoot underneath the scorching rays of the naked sun.

But just as

the heat becomes unbearable the soothing breeze of Tony and Charlie's beats and atmosphere blows a soothing breeze and returns you back to the original view point, all through the lense

Words: A-Cyde

7 8 Auxiliary weight 9

Runaways

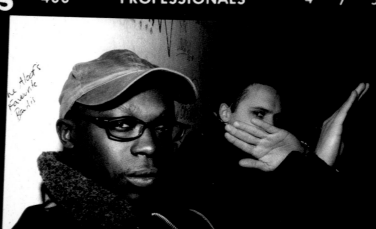

To some the tu
worldwide hav
years or so.
wherby recor
under the ne
developed bec
expression. Th
own right
rythmic ph
We hope

0A 1

4000

The Turntable

[...] may represent outdated technology, but in contrast DJ's
[...] developing the use of this equipment for the last twenty
[...] pioneers of the 'scratching' and 'cutting' techniques,
[...] manipulated using the hands moving back and fourth
[...] create new and unique sounds, these techniques have
[...] more complex and elaborate. allowing greater degrees of
[...] elevated the turntable's position into an instrument in it's
[...] ve used the turntable to create melodic lead lines,
[...] d special effects all interlocked to the arrangements.
[...] e contributed to the use of the turntables as a new
and exciting sound.

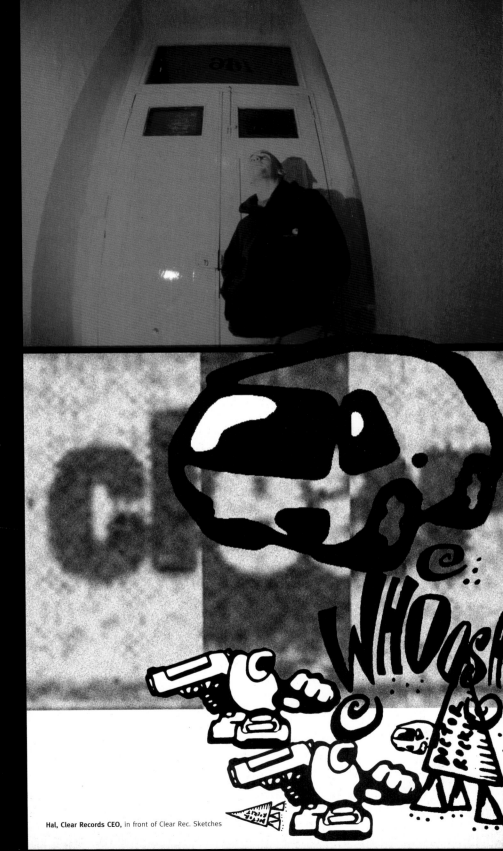

Hal, Clear Records CEO, in front of Clear Rec. Sketches

sporsche

porsche porsche

wieviele wehrlose Igel
haben diese kalten Felgen
schon überfahren?

Montag 23.00 Uhr. Ein Tag wie jeder andere oder zumindest genau das.
Tunakan und Pulsinger sitzen mit uns in Pulsingers Villa im Weste
Pulsinger trinkt Waldmeisterbrause und Tunakan Türkischen Mok
Der Kamin lodert und im Hintergrund läuft Countrymusic.
Patrick wirkt ein wenig nervös heute, er sagt, es muß am Wetter
Er trommelt permanent auf seinem Körper oder dem Sessel.
Tunakan ist super relaxt, er scheint fast zu schlafen.
Er hat ein paar Blättchen in den Händen und sucht irgendetwas in

2740   4

Er trommelt perm82

Tunakan ist super r

Er hat ein paa Blä

Lodown: Ok, seid Ihr soweit?
Pulsinger: Klar, klar, kann losgehen.
Lodown: Wie ist es eigentlich, Patrick Pulsinger zu sein ?
Tunakan: Stressig !
Lo: Und umgekehrt ?
P: Ich glaube, es ist extrem chillig, Erdem zu sein.
Lo: Wo wollt ihr hin in Eurem Leben?
T: Eine eigene Wohnung. Patrick hat ja diese Villa hier, aber ich muß mit meinem
Vater zusammen wohnen. Mein Vater lacht immer so laut - das hört man durch die
Wand. Er lacht die ganze Zeit und wenn er nicht lacht, dann schnarcht er.
P: Ich könnte eine größere Garage und vielleicht noch zwei, drei Autos gebrauchen.
Lo: Warum gebt ihr ausgerechnet Lodown ein Exclusiv-Interview?
P: Wegen der Kohle, die Ihr uns gegeben habt, außerdem ist das gar kein
Exclusiv-Interview, gleich kommen die Leute von Bild-Zeitung und Frontpage.
Lo: Man erzählt sich, daß Ihr auf Viva eine Sendung machen sollt ?
P: Ach, ja? Wir haben schon eine auf Fm 4, da ziehen sich in jeder Sendung
die Mädels aus..
Lo: Also keine Techno-Gala-Show mit Heike Makatsch, Marusha und Euch beiden?
P: Es gibt Pläne für eine TV-Show mit Toni Polster und Burt Reynolds, aber
darüber
verraten wir noch nichts.
Lo: Ihr zählt zu den heißesten Playboys im Showbusiness und die Frauen
liegen Euch nur so zu Füßen. Laßt uns ´mal ein paar Inside-Storys hören.
T: Soviel habt Ihr uns ja auch wieder nicht gezahlt.
Lo: Wobei wird Euch schlecht ?
T: Wenn Orel seine Schuhe auszieht.
P: Design von neuen Autos.
Lo: Patrick, Du hast ja mehrere Autos, welches bevorzugst Du zur Zeit?P:
Käfer Cabrio, mit 2,8 Liter Porsche Motor, und was man sonst so brauch´ in
einem California Custom Bug.
Lo: Ich finde, Deine Felgen sehen irgendwie prollig aus.
(Pulsinger geht beleidigt aus dem
Zimmer)
T: Ja mich kotzen die Felgen auch an. Ich
muß sie ja immer donnerstags polieren.
Lo: Hast Du manchmal Angst wenn Patrick zu
schnell fährt?
T: Ja und wie, bei 230 klappert der Kübel so laut,
daß man denkt er fliegt auseinander.
Lo: Welche Projekte stehen an ?
T:Wir gehen im Mai, mit den Leuten von Clear Records
auf Europa Tournee und es gibt
Releases : Sluts and Strings LP ! Und Showroom
Recordings #2.
Lo: Wie sieht die Zukunft der Clubmusic aus ?
P: Sehr differenziert !
Lo:Wie war das in der Zeit, als Ihr noch nicht im
Showbusiness wart und euch Eure
Prostitution und Drogenhandel verdienen mußtet?
T: Hart, aber herzlich.
Lo: Als was würdet Ihr am liebsten reinkarnieren?
P: Als Kakteen.
Lo: Was würdet Ihr tun, wenn Ihr wüßtet, Ihr hättet
nur noch 15 Minuten zu leben?
T: Chillen bis zum Schluß.
Lo: Habt ihr Sex miteinander?
P:...In mageren Zeiten weiß man nie
...Prinzipiell Nein.

Empfangen von: 8178996
17-MRZ-96 21:46   CHEAP ENTERTAINMENT   8178996   17/03/96 22:48   S.: 1
SEITE: 1

BENETTON
UNITED
TUNAKAN
THOUGHT
LORS

passe auf Ihre Kinder auf!
niedriger Stundensatz!VEA

mark broom

[Adventures into Techno]

[Mark Broom´s Musiker Karriere beginnt im Studio von Blackdog.
Ja, ihr habt richtig gelesen – bei den legendären Blackdog Boys.
Mark, damals noch Fahrradmessenger, war ihr Studiohivi, der Assistent, der die Kabel stöpselt, den Kaffe macht und die Joints dreht.
Wie man sieht, scheint Mark nicht nur diese Aufgaben bewältigt zu haben – nein er hat auch immer schön aufgepaßt, wenn Ed und Andy von Ed´s, Effekten, Samples und Basslines sprachen und an diesen rumbastelten.

Wie das Schicksal halt so spielt waren Ed und Andy zu einer Studiosession nicht erschienen und der wartende Mark kochte vor Langeweile literweise Kaffee und drehte haufenweise Joints, bis es ihm einfach zu öde wurde und er den Sampler anschmiß.
Als Ed und Andy am nächsten Tag die über Nacht entstandenen Tracks von Mark hörten, waren sie mächtig beeindruckt und wir dürfen uns auf eine weitere, demnächst erscheinende Folge der Midnight Funk Essentials freuen.

Mittlerweile hat Mark ca. 50 Tracks veröffentlicht, ein eigenes Label mit dem Namen Pure Plastik am Laufen und er steht kurz davor seine erste LP auf Pure Plastik zu veröffentlichen.
Daß er musikalisch sehr variationsreich agieren kann, bewies er nicht zuletzt durch seine Releases und Remixes auf Mo´Wax
James Lavelle sagt über Mark Broom: "Mark ist einer der talentiertesten Producer in London zur Zeit.
Ich vergleiche ihn gerne mit Carl Craig. Wenn Mark seinen Weg als Producer und Remixer weiter verfolgt, wie bisher, dann hat er mit Sicherheit noch eine große Zukunft vor sich."
Das haben auch einige andere bemerkt und Warp-Records wird ein Projekt von ihm und seinem Studiopartner Dave Hill veröffentlichen, das den Titel "Symplectic" trägt.
Es gab auch bereits einige Angebote von Majors aber Mark sagt dazu:
Ich bin absolut nicht an einem Major-Deal interessiert,
die wollen doch nur den Hype absucken und dann wirst Du fallengelassen, wenn die Verkaufszahlen nicht mehr stimmen.
Für mich sind Verkaufszahlen absolut sekundär. Klar freue ich mich, wenn der Verkauf einer Platte die Produktion finanziert und wenn vielleicht noch ein paar Pfund abfallen – fantastisch, dann kann ich mir neues Equipment kaufen.
Primär ist es wichtig für mich, daß ich meine Musik machen kann, was zu fressen im Kühlschrank habe und ein wenig Gras zum Chillen. Ich bin ein sehr bescheidener Mensch.
Mark ist auch als Producer sehr bescheiden.
Man könnte auch minimalistisch sagen, denn seine Sounds wählt er akribisch aus und verwendet sie sehr sparsam.

Ein weiteres Markenzeichen sind seine aufwendig editierten Drum Breaks.
Zuletzt verpaßte Mark Nicolette einen smoothen Elektro Remix für "Beautiful Day" auf Talkin Loud.

In einer Zeit, in der sich House und Techno umorientieren müssen ist Mark auf jeden Fall an vorderster Front
und sorgt permanent für neue Impulse
und wir dürfen uns wohl noch auf
einen ganzen Haufen innovativer Releases von ihm freuen.

So watch out for Mark Broom!

→ cross at green
(for positive seen)

10:15P THURSDA
03.27.97 2152

I always told her
...but sh

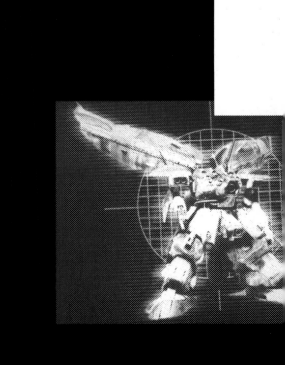

μⁱ°© f threethousand plus
the robotsoul emphasis
elektrogeknarrze

"There are no limits and boundaries in Drum & Bass. You can bring in any kind of vibe into this music, that's what we try to do, not just sampling old shit, but creating new vibes, even if it is a Heavy Metal vibe. As long as you do it right and sensibly, it works. It's just a melting pot, where you bring a lot of things into, without copying blatantly, I mean that's at least what we try." – **Danny Breaks / February 1997**

Drum & Bass - 21rd century soul for the masses?

"What drum & bass means to me? It's as simple as drum, bass, rhythms, fast tempo, coming somewhere from rave music, house, techno, hip hop and jazz...Beat cipher about 150 b.p.m., based on rhythm, that's about all there is!"

Photek, the most widely recognized genius of modern breakbeat music, is right. Drum & Bass should be all about the infectious legacy of the bass and the breaks, about spine-tingling nights in pitch black smoke filled clubs, where hundreds of people shuffle to the bassline. But it isn't! Not in 1998, not with people like Goldie or Roni Size around. The underground phenomenon people were laughing at only a few years ago has surfaced to the forefront of the international popculture. Drum & bass is hip as fuck; mainly thanks to Goldie, the first and only real drum & bass superstar. Even in their most lucid dreams a team of top marketing executives could not have concocted the Goldie phenomenon. He was like a gift from heaven when he became the face for the largely faceless jungle scene and spearheaded a breakbeat revolution that hasn't stopped since. Today, he is an international celebrity, dating popstars and supermodels, working with the likes of Noel Gallagher, David Bowie and the Blastermaster KRS 1, scheming films with Val Kilmer and gracing international title pages more often than Madonna and Michael Jackson together! This, however, is only the one side of drum & bass. The other, very well reflected by Ronni Size and his Bristol posse, is about steady innovation, about taking the music to the next level, about creating new forms of aural landscapes, and yes indeed, about winning the Mercury Prize. Well, and after taking home Britain's most prestigious music trophy against the likes of the Prodigy, Radiohead and the Spice Girls, Ronni Size made sure that drum & bass had finally established itself in the mainstream of the international music scene. Now, five, six years after the sonic boom first hit the UK underground, the music has been commercialised massively, and today every fucker and his little brother listens to Ed Rush, Optical or Photek. The mainstream press and people who wouldn't even know about it a year ago just cannot ignore this genre-breaking sound anymore. Drum & bass has been one of the biggest urban success stories´ Britain has experienced in the last few years. As a culture spawned from a strange mix of new sounds and styles, drum & bass has been on the rise since the early 90s when the music was called jungle. The culture and community that has been growing in the shadows of London's, Bristol's and Wolverhampton's ugly council estates is now so diverse that it is extremely difficult to categorize. The lexicon of genre specific terms, once used as a sort of tongue-in cheek description has been co-opted for use in regular sentences for regular people. Words like Techstep, Darkcore, Jazzy Jungle, Jump Up, Bristol sound are now all too common in mainstream publications, employing journalists who don't have a clue what they are writing about. Today drum & bass is a worldwide sound and movement, and after England, Germany is the second strongest breeding ground. Labels like Don Q Records, Precision, Case Invaders, U.S.E./Offroad and Groove Attack and DJs and producers like DJ Blowpipe, Bassface Sascha and Panacea are no strangers to the London dons anymore. However, the sound's bastardisation has taken extreme forms and some tracks sound more like a sonic assault on people's eardrums. "It's good to see the growth of a healthy scene all over the place," Goldie reckons. "But some of the boys are fuckin' too hard. They got to chill a bit more on their production, just take it easy, you know." As the music spreads all over the planet, it doesn't seem to be a coincidence that the hype is somewhat apocalyptic, almost foretelling of the doom ahead as well as the hope of streets paved with gold. This in fact might have been the reason for the first big catfights within the scene: Goldie's engineer and Moving Shadow label honcho Rob Playford sacked halfway through the production of the golden man's epic "Saturn'z Return", Cleveland Watkiss left his Metalheadz residency, Kemi & Storm sacked from Metalheadz, but soon reinstated again, Moving Shadow's complete label personell walked out... Shit like this happens, no doubt, but the way it happened, all the bitchin' and nasty things quoted by the press made you wonder if the internal 25/8 stress and the permanent jetlag have fucked up some headz. "To tell you the truth, we ain't no time for that bullshit, that's their business," oldschool pioneer and leading light Dego aka 4 Hero admits. "But it's sad, 'cos they are the flagship for the scene. It's the most premiere label of the whole thing, and it's about time that some people focus again more on what is really important." But despite all the problems and the unstoppable commercialisation this music still combines a beautiful diversity and ass-whipping energy . Of all the producers, a few stand out, and there are four or five camps that completely rule the business: Roni Size and the Bristol bunch (V, Full Cycle, Talkin Loud) with completely mindblowing breakbeat adaptions of soul, jazz, funk and acid, and some amazing vocal tracks, the one and only Grooverider (Prototype, Metalheadz, Sony) with techno drones for the next millenium and quality remixes in quadriple packs, Lemon D. and Dillinja (Valve, Pain, London, R&S, Metalheadz) with their unmistakable analogue jazz-fuelled lo-fi, high-rise inner city sound, Photek and the Source Direct (Virgin, Metalheadz) boys with sounds from another planet and Optical & Technical Itch (Prototype, Metalheadz, 31 Records, Virus) with a hard, twisted and anti-conformist future sound. Apart from that Johnny L came back with an amazing box set, Doc Scott still bangs out anthem after anthem, the Trouble on Vinyl and Rennegade Hardware camp represents in style and 4-Hero was already a step ahead of the rest. Like back in the days when the whole drum & bass/jungle saga started in a small Dollis Hill bedroom. Reinforced's Marc Mac "When I look at the whole scope of drum & bass, I sometimes sit back and think 'Shit, it's gone so far, 'cos there was a time when there was four of us sitting in the bedroom upstairs, speeding up breaks. It was only four people in the world doing it. Gus, Ian, Dego and me. The fact that it has gone so big now, does seem a little weird sometimes. But it still needs to travel further and shouldn't come to a standstill. That's why we try everything to push it."

CREATURE SOUND

Sunday night, Hoxton Square, Old Street, crews of youth
roll from all sides of England to congregate together
within this one space for the duration of this, the drum
and bass sermon at the metalheadz session.
Preachers like Grooverider, Fabio, Photek and Roni Size
make their way down into the chamber beneath the entrance,
to then find themselves in an environment that feels like
a windtunnel of sounds.
The dance in it's foetal stage.
This foetus that's still to grow and define itself, in
this dark, aquatic space. It is a foetus of syncopated
rhythms which beat you to a trance; a bastard music, with
a diverse and spiritual following.
Freight weight bass rushes up and around.
Hyper-ballistic breaks blast through the venue. In the
hearts and minds of the crowd, you can see a rush of liquid
fire.
The vibe is present, a vibe which hits hard but yields no
pain.
The drum and bass winds up the heads, the MC's chat
ceaselessly to a crowd, eager to experience new visions
of sonic paths through the concrete jungle.
For even though it's just a dance and the music can be
deemed as noise,
it demands you to move and it demands you to distort your
senses and your perception.

FABIO

D.J.   STRETCH

Within these dark chambers of wall to wall sound, voices
carried from 24 kilo watt amplifiers, dub bass, drums, sweat,
heat, feverous passion; one hardly imagines above in the cold
world, the realities of life.
This is the music of the unsafe and unsure. The movement of
youth who find society too rigid for their bodies of fluid
and tissue. Dancing in this red womb you feel safe, you feel
maybe, as you contemplate, red eyed and blunted, that you can
believe in yourself and conquer the world.

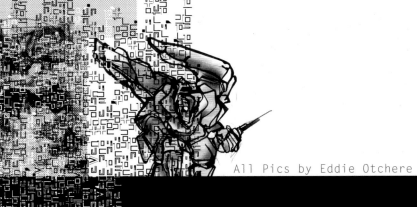

Goldie: Drum and Bass is the only way for me at the moment to express my thoughts.
When I'm writing a tune I think of a picture, an image and then I transfer it to music.
It's about youth, changing your environment and believing in the future.

JUNGLIST GALS

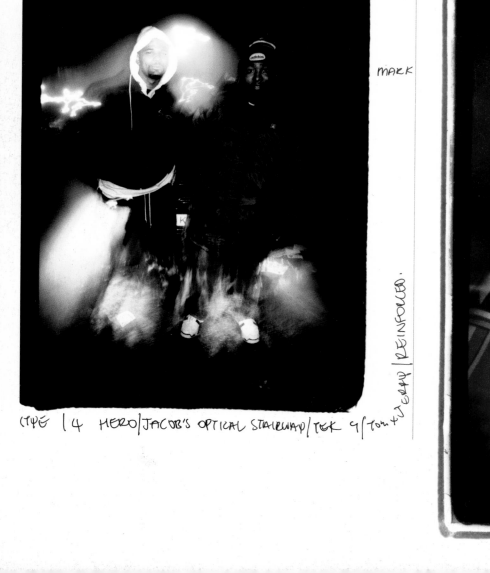

MARK

TYPE | 4 HERO/JACOB'S OPTICAL STAIRWAY/TEK 9/TOM + JERRY/REINFORCED.

Grooverider: Drum and Bass has been our path to victory.
We have to stick together to reach our full potential.
With Goldie I could see some major progress, same thing with Fabio,
Bukem, Photek and now Dillinja and tomorrow Ed Rush.
It's like the Zulu Nation, a growing force.

this two pages clockwise: **Hidden Agenda, 4 Hero, Dillinja, Digital and Photek**

サントラQ

SOUND TRACK
QUEST
9

CONCERNING
PHOTEK

rouble on vinyl

renegade hardware

GENOTYPE

trouble on vinyl

"Drum & bass is that original Roy Ayers jazz sound. The breaks are jazz breaks. Yeah, we're just another generation of jazz musicians."

Götz Werner takes a look at Lemon D, the futuristic funkforce of drum & bass music, and how he is looking for new challenges for 1998 and beyond....

"This year a lot of the funky stuff comes through, and hopefully we get some more girls back in the clubs, 'cos right now there are a lot of trainspotters that just stand at the decks. It's too hard and noone wants to listen to that shit all night...If you do things at a slower pace more people can get into it. You open your sound up to more people, you get more music and feeling in there!"
Lemon D is finally ready. He is about to drop his debut album, with an interactive CD-Rom on R&S records and to start his own ground-breaking Valve club night with mate, loft neighbour and audio sparring partner Dillinja. But more so, the 25-year old Kevin King is ready to rewrite the blueprint of drum & bass music and define a whole new aspirational mood in drum & bass; one that captures his own, very personal spirit of urban London. A spirit defined by his hard but groovy sound - influenced by musicians like Sonnie Liston, Roy Ayers, James Brown and West Coast hip hop - fantastic drum programming, psychedellic analogue sequences, pulverised basslines and extremely edgy and diverse beats, sampled, chopped and looped to his very unique futuristic and fresh funk & bass feast.

Despite recording a dazzling array of cuts for all the top drum & bass labels including Metalheadz, Prototype, V-Recordings, R&S Records and his own imprints Valve and Pain,
he's been keeping a low profile, watching the scene from the outside rather than being involved with everyone and everything. And he registered with growing concern what happened to the music he breathes, loves and lives since 1991. "The whole scene should be a melting pot where you hear a lot of different things, but when you go to most clubs these days, it's just one sound and you think 'fuckin' hell man, what's the time, I better go home now'. It's gone up his own arse, but if everyone would do his own thing, there would be much more colour in the scene." With some of the shining lights of this scene heavily engaged in bickering with each other and fighting for the biggest piece of the extremely lucrative cake, Kevin is glad

that he kept his nose out of the trouble. He just doesn't want to get caught into the ridiculous drum & bass politics. He is in it for the music, and that's it. "It's my life, but it's not, otherwise it gets too shitty. I'm not into that", he explains with a serious look. "At the end of the day, I get a phone call and that's it. I don't really know all the ins and outs, I don't see Goldie that much, I'm not signed to Metalheadz, I've done stuff for them, I got a lot of recognition through Metalheadz, but at the end of the day I am an artist in my own right."

That's exactly what he wants and will be remembered as - an artist in his own right, someone who always sustained a sparkingly intense and innovative vision that kept surprising and delighting in equal measures. In these weeks, you can expect guns to be blazing, as a few of the dons ride into town and release their major label albums. But one thing can be assured. Lemon D's shit will stand out, one way or the other. The amount of work and patience he's put into his music is unreal; like Photek and only a few other producers all the breaks on his album are completely produced by himself; no cheap sampling and chopping up. But now, after troublesome months with computer breakdowns, lost samples, sleepless nights, endless recording sessions with live musicians and fights with his longtime girlfriend, one of the greatest pieces of drum & bass music looks ready to attack your eardrums. Hard Amen tracks, passing sounds of sport car engines, strange dictaphone and fax machine sounds, futuristic funk excursions and a lot of down tempo tracks at 110 and 120 b.p.m. promise as much pleasure as the interactive CD-Rom with Super-8 clips, hidden samples and other gimmicks, and the Valve club night which will push drum & bass clubs with its idea of different theme zones into unknown realms.

The future looks bright for the 25 year old all round, multi-skilled engineer, producer, programmer and breakbeat excursionist. But despite all the acclaim and hype that surround him, Kevin, the King of the Castle is as chilled as ever. "You know, we don't sit there and brag about things like others do", he says with a cheeky grin when exactly in that second a massive bassline reverberates from Dillinja's neighbouring loft. "We take it easy, focus on our music and wait, 'cos the real bomb is still to drop yet!"

fotos eddie otchere

tribute

a
to... ...blowing odyssey miles & his buddies
cleared on bitches brew decades ag...

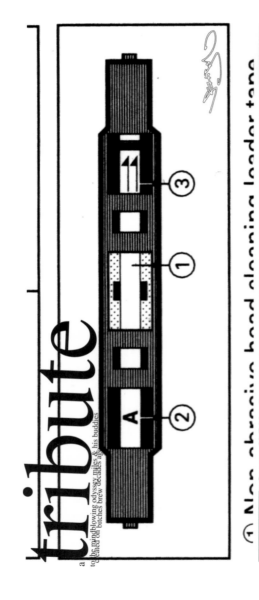

11

A

① ② ③

① Non abrasive head cleaning leader tape

CCSLP 243

MILES DAVIS

1. MILES RUNS THE VOODOO DOWN
(M. Davis) Warner Chappell Music Ltd.

℗ 1970 CBS Records Inc.

Licensed from CBS Records (UK) Ltd.
The copyright in this sound recording
is owned by CBS Records Inc.

Made in England

33⅓ RPM
RECORD 2

PERFORMANCE AND BROADCASTING OF THIS RECORD PROHIBITED

... PUBLIC PERFORMANCE. LENDING. HIRING. UNAUTHORISED COPYING RESERVED REPRODUCED THE WORK OF THE OWNER OF THE WORK ... PRODUCER AND OF THE OWNER OF THE WORK REPRODUCED RESERVED UNAUTHORISED COPYING

nICKgomez

New York's Finest Guerilla Filmmaker

'Completely economic devices. 16mm. 12 days. $35,000 budget.' Economics influenced the look of 'Laws of Gravity' writer-director Nick Gomez refers to the realistic look of his debut feature film starring Peter Greene and Adam Trese as two lowlifes struggling through New York, culminating in Trese's fatalistic death. 'Laws of Gravity' was an unexpected, critically acclaimed independent success. Generally handheld cinematography, staccato editing and improvised diologues created a semi-documtary, cinema direct look that set new standards in the 'Mean Street' genre and wowed critics and festival-goers worldwide. The compelling hood flic electrifies with to his authentic characterization and its sensible street knowledge, avoiding gang-related stereotypes. The shaved-headed Gomez didn't intend to flatter critics or trend-sucking audiences. Simply the lack of money made 'Laws of Gravity' a superb low-key artventure. 'Bigger budgets come with more technical opportunities and - probably - more fun. The more money you spend, the slicker the look's gonna be'.

Teaming up with Gramercy Pictures and Spike Lee as executive producer, Nick Gomez was able to work with a respectable budget for his second movie. 'New Jersey Drive' deals with joyriding adoloscents in Newark. Based on a true incidence Gomez depicted the ill-fated carchases of underprivileged kids and cops. 'It's a fuckin Indy 500 around there' Gomez was told during principal photography. 'NJ Drive' is pessimistic portrait of the current situation of urban life. His protagonists use their criminal activities as the only possibile way to escape from a socially imposed trap. 'It's the lack of opportunity out there, and there's great deal of social and political oppression as well. These towns look like they're occupied by the police. Stealing cars is a form of rebellion for these guys - no different than the kids who tag or skateboard around. It's a way for them to have their own voice, to show their skills. To do something that has, to them, some value.'

A character-driven, fueled story about rising problems in projects and the frustrated inhabitants coping with their harsh reality. 'NJ Drive' reveals the main preoccupation of this intense filmmaker, the development of authentic, edgy characters.

'That's what I'm interested in. Characters, kinda frontier living. They have to create their own rules, because they're living apart from society's standards. Basic and pure.' Formerly working with Shooting Gallery's Hal Hartley, Nick Gomez brings the focus on controversial characters and loyality. Perhaps according to own Irish-Italian upbringing in Boston, including frequentyouthful arrests.

The theme of loyality is also pervasive in his third cinematic project, titled 'illtown'. Set in Miami, Florida, Nick Gomez left New York to direct an elusive film about wealthy drug dealers who intend to quit their lucrative job to lead a normal life. Hunted by guilty conscience and his betrayed partner, Michael Rappaport as the main protagonist fails to escape his surroundings. All involved persons seem to be determined , unable to do what they originally wanted. 'It's the eternal battle. I tried to use to various religious and literary references. The characters are related to certain associations. You know what's intended. But I liked the idea that the characters don't have to exist, actually. They could be dead.' Nick Gomez says. 'It hasn't to be a gothic vision of the other world. I like Florida because of the bright, intense colors. It's hard to make New York look surreal.'

Therefore 'illtown' is an elegiac down-tempo drug experience. A stunning, but exhausting film. 'I used this film as a ladder to climb out of an hole I was trapped in. It was a theraphy. A relation splitted. I took too much drugs. I didn't care about anything.'

'illtown' is the last part of his trilogy that shows a dark, urban world filled with guns, drugs and violence. Basically buddy-movies. 'Obviously, all three pieces are genre films, containing gangsters, buddies, girls and druglords. TV-movies on drugs.'

This dedicated, independent filmmaker progresses with further projects.

'I'll do Hollywood movies - and sell out!!!' Nick Gomez laughs.

'I'm planning a adaption of a novel called 'Suicide'. It's about five gorgeous sister who commit suicide. And nobody knows why. It's a comedy. It's funny. The girls are too beautiful to live and too young to die. Another screenplay I'm developing right now is named 'Pressure Drop'. Kind of a Western on the Virgin Islands. Cocaine cowboys, washed-up CIA assassins and a lot of whackiness.'

'There some themes that I want to explore, issues that I want to raise. the point of making a movie is to create different realities for the audience to step into. Even if the method - that you're using to tell the story in a realistic way - employs devices like handheld cameras and improvised dialogues. That's still a device. You're manipulating your audience.'

line. 'There's this place; it's a factory and you don't know what the fuck goes on there. But you put your money in one end and your cassette comes out the other.' This engineering method was successful. In the late 8oies and early 9oies, Propaganda, evidently, dominates the visual appearance of MTV. Aerosmith's Janie's Got A Gun and several Madonna vids were directed by the innovative hotshot Fincher. 'I wanted to experiment with all techniques available, to work with the freshest materials. Actually, I wasn't interested in the music.'
It took four years until Fincher came back to the big screen. 1995, the macabre Se7en was a surprising hit. From his commercial work Fincher transported his dark, neon-lit settings to a feature film. But it wasn't the exclusively the look of Se7en that makes this morbid thriller a must-see. Andrew Kevin Walker's perfect screenplay was stunningly written.
'I like scripts where I don't know how they gonna end. The storyline has to be unpredictable such as Andrew Kevin Walker's piece of work. I read his script till I got to that scene, in which John Doe, the religious serial-killer, give himself up to the police. I took the script, looked at it and went like 'Oh, there are still 100 pages to read.' It's a great story with unexpected plot-twists. It starts as a cop-buddy-movie, features classical thriller elements and concludes in a horror-movie ending.'
The off-beat ending was the issue of permanent discussions throughout pre-production. Compared to regular Hollywood endings, this one was too offensive, too nihilistic. But Brad Pitt insisted on the doing the film with the original final scene featuring Gwyneth Paltrow's head delivered via parcel services. David Fincher also tested his power of persuasion.
'I told my producer that we're going to shoot a classic. Twenty years from now, people having a party will be talking about an old film like 'I don't know the title anymore. But do you remember this one scene this girl's head is send in a box to the cops. That was cruel.' So we decided to keep the original version.'
Resulting in a masterpiece, Fincher combines his visual intensity with Walker's well elaborated characters and dramatic construction. Imaginary Forces provided the distracing credit titles, using End of Print - typography and reversing the usual direction, the credits roll from the top to the bottom of the screen.
Nevertheless. To be honest. In general, I don't like my films. It's impossible. During post-production you watch your film about 1,300 times - over and over again. You've seen the material and the reels. You've seen the tape on the actors' coats. You've seen it all. You find a great script that intrigues you. But you ruin that script for ever.
As a kid I used to watch movies and asked myself 'Why did the fucking director do this, why did he do that?' And now I'm doing the same with my own movies. What a fuckin idiot. Why did I do this?'
David Fincher recently released his third movie 'The Game'. A distracting puzzle where Michael Douglas looses control over his life. It's a massive manipulation, semi-scientology style.
'Michael Douglas' character is similar to Ted Turner. Happy-go-lucky, well-balanced, handles all the situations in life, a self made millionaire. He limited his contacts, therefore he limits all possible amount of chaos. He has total controll over his life. All over sudden, the people conspiraly fuck him over in two hours and, finally, go 'happy birthday'.
At one point in my life I felt guilty of making my life effortless, make it run easier. I had my assistants. Lost touch with real life. For years I worked hard to gain respect, to be cool. I tried to cultivate this behaviour, tried to act responsibly. The greatest lesson in life was the birth of my daughter. She didn't show any interest in me a minute and pissed on me. I was in world domination, make my big company and my little daughter pisses on me.'
Michael Douglas felt the same way. He shut his office at Paramount, he got divorced. He wanted to act, do something that puts him back into the race. He could relate to the situation his character is trapped in.'
The process Michael Douglas' character goes to, including his change in behavior and his growing empathy with other people is similar to the process of developing a screenplay or constructing a film in general. Considering the connection, the screenwriter or director is the master puppets who leads the actor to a certain destination. The Game is a metaphor about building sets in which the protagonist journeys to reach a higher level in education and attitude towards other people. This certain process is still under influence of other unpredictable elements.
'At the end of our shooting Michael Douglas asked the waitress Deborah Unger where she came from. She replied 'Oklahoma, ah Colorado.' Deborah just fucked up her lines. It wasn't part of the script. It was great. It fitted. That's how improvisation or mistakes improve the movie.
Actually, Jody Foster wanted to play the waitress. Yeah, great. Oscar-winning Jody Foster pours a drink on Michael Douglas, Really, it would be a big surprise, revealing at the end, that waitress Jody Foster was part of the whole conspiration. Yeah, sure. I didn't know Deborahs Ungers work before. But she has a tremendous physical appeerence. She isn't girly. She's a real stud. Solid and tough. She's chain-smokin'. And she can even spit. She's a career waitress.'

Watching the scene with that new improvised part, I thought great. Fascinating acting techniques. Impressing. Then I saw the scene in the cafeteria and I went like 'Holy shit. I'm a total idiot!' About 8o extras were gathered in that room. I'd better put 10 or 12 important persons in there to achieve the necessary effect. But you learn by doing.' Fincher assures.
'That's why I continue working on music videos and TV advertising. It's the best way to experiment with specific technologies. I love the process of making commercials. I just don't like to deal with the people who manage this stuff. I'm fascinated by people who are video-saffy. People who know what to do. Just like Spike Jonze (who's done videos for Björk, Pharcyde and the legendary 'Sabotage' piece for the Beastie Boys and co-owns L.A. based Girl Skateboards.) 'I dig Spike Jonze. He has also a cameo part in The Game. Joining with video artists we created the pre-credit scenes and the flashbacks. 16mm reverse material, normally used for video clips, blown up to 35mm. Then we put the material into the sun, drove over it with a car. Cleaned it the last time and put it into an optical printer. And copied again. It was fun, made it look like trash.'
These shots produce the impression of real, obsolete Super8 material. Whereas all Fincher flics were dominated by dark and deep colors. Due to contracts the film distribution firms are liable to develope the copies twice. Expensive. But that's an artistic experience David Fincher made directing commercials. Fincher and his fellow Propaganda mates are technically proficient, with an unique visual flourish. Critic still claims that Propaganda denies narrative, interesting characters or content. Propaganda is the big budget Ponderosa with horses like Con Air, The Rock or Replacement Killers. Most of them are slick adrenalin-flics without the slightest educational message but lots of explosives and stereotypes, custom-made for the MTV audience. On the other hand Propaganda film laboratory approaches filmmaking with a new credo. 'If you can tell a story in 3 and half minutes, the regular commercial presentation time, you can tell a story within the length of a feature film'. Sometimes this leads to conventional story-telling covered with pure action roller-coaster elements. On the otherhand they come with fresh re-definitions of old genre standards like the action feast, comic-style Neo-Western Con Air written by Scott Rosenberg or David Fincher's Se7en. 'I didn't want to go the filmschool. I didn't know what the point was.' explains David Fincher. 'Nobody knows nothing.'

david fincher

'Nobody knows nothing. There is no formular to direct a movie.'
David Fincher made that experience while working for special-fx-factory ILM, making countless music videos and TV-commercials for his co-owned company Propaganda Films and, finally, directing part 3 of the Alien franchise, the intriguing tech noir serial-killer final Se7en and the subtle manipulation-thriller The Game.
'You know, the point of filmmaking is that your producing a prototype. It's designed to fly, but it hasn't before. And noone knows if this prototype will ever fly. You've got this blueprint, an idea. Your script and principal photography. Actually the first time you watch your movie is about four months before the movie is released. That's the time you spent all your money.
However, three weeks before we started shooting Alien3 I already knew, I fucked up the whole movie. I allowed the executives of 20th century to give me piecemeal money. Piecemeal money to build the set. So I destroyed the first essential of an Alien movie. I had many rooms, the chappel, the cells, spreaded all over the studio's facility. I couldn't move with the camera from one room into the other. And that's the most important point for a horror-house-movie every Alien film is based on.'
David Fincher, back then in his early twenties, was responsible for the lowest-grossing installment of the famous Alien franchise.
He started his unorthodox cinema-carrier creating mate-painting and miniatures for George Lucas' leading special effects factory ILM. Here he was involved in the production of the Star Wars episodes IV and V, The Empire Strikes Back and Return of the Jedi, and Indiana Jones as well. With a huge technical experience David Fincher left Lucas to do commercials and music videos. Fincher co-founded Propaganda Films. His original vision of Propaganda's function was similar to an assembly

marius sommer and sami harithi sequences
are included for only 29.99, what a bargain!

flach seq.

a visual enjoyment, just like lodown.

my car
is flyer than
yours prod. 97

superflos. a videoproduction by lodown mag. called
a lotec. lofi visual joint

SUPER

SCREAM 18 20H30 23
02 SUPERLO8 SAT 23
LEBEN IN ROSAROT
14H NON STOP ANIMATIONEN

SUPERLO8

boarding, thrills & entertainment

LO8

Münster, June 1997 997

wieder.
...grossver-
...zur
...jugendkultur.
urban guerilla
...nicht zur
...nach berlin.

er trancet und gabbert nicht
irgedwo auf rügen und goat sich auch nicht in der kieler heide rum.
ihm sind bizarre pop komm's egal. er interrailt nicht durch sizilien oder
airravet auf die malediven gegen ende juni packt er
vielmehr seinen rucksack mit drei t-shirts für die kommenden vier wochen,
verlässt sein 12m²-loft in budapest und skatet die nächsten 16 tage über bratislava,
hof und essen nach münster zum worldcup. wenn er dann dort der einzige aus ungarn
ist, darf er wahrscheinlich sogar starten. danach muss er sich beeilen, um rechtzeitig
nach london zu kommen. vielleicht nimmt ihn dann
irgendein italiener mit zum mystic-cup nach prag und zur
...nach wien – kassel ist er dann ja auch schon fast wieder zu hause.
wir haben das auch so gemacht. am 26. juni haben wir uns morgens um 3 getroffen, alex
...beim doper vertrunstück und sind dann losgeskatet. unser fotograf, alex
...hatte die nacht durchgemacht und sein board bis big eden vergessen.
kurzerhand ist er dann mit dem klapprad seiner mutter gefahren. bei kassel hatten
wir uns mit markus verabredet, der sich   in der zeit vertan hatte und eine woche

patryk:
jesce polska nie zagnela

game:
i will land this one.
i will land this one.
i will.
i will.

julie: he ll better
stick this one.

chad:
i can't wait to
light another fatty!

julie: he ll
stick this one

lance: damn –
this sport is still
so fuckin
sick.

mike: shit - i forgot my trick
donny: shit - i forgot my trick...

eric:
did i really close the kitchenwindow
back at home?

moses:
if i can get a hand on that guy who stole
my equipment – they ll accuse me of murder.

Darstellungsform: 1c [B/W]
Darstellungsform: 4c [CMYK]

heath:
still wrestling with the
...stion whether or not i should
...nge my clothes next week.
...well, maybe i do! or not?

Münster, June 1997 997

C+Y   Y   Y+M   M   C+M   C   W   C+M+Y   Bk

mike:
is it only me or is anybody else
feeling dizzy here?!?

donny:
ed will love me for
representing toy
machine in this pic

ronnie:
i hope, this graphic-design-jerk at lodown
will put me together the right way –
but then again: i don't care 'bout it anyway!

zu früh in hamburg losgefahren
und war somit vier tage zu früh in kassel. in münster angekommen, staunten wir nicht schlecht: titus liess sich nach letztjährigem
desaster nicht lumpen und baute ein ...en männer-streetcourse. allen hat alles sehr gut gefallen. alex hat dann markus, sam und

mark:
it's all about jumpin on cars!

joey:
it's all about filming it!

chet:
this sure will be a bomb of a pic.

helge:
...st mein 645003... skatebig.

L. LONDON

america teaming up at the cups, f.l.t.r. rudy johnson, unknown, eric koston, wade speyer, kareem campbell and mike carroll.

sam:
alter - wie locker is
das denn!

till:

robert auf den lenker genommen und fuhr mit den jungs nach london. dort hat´s auch allen sehr gut gefallen und alex hat sehr schöne photografien gemacht. alles war sehr schön und auch gut.

rozen moments - flachphotographics
isual mayhem & ausgeführte rechtschreibreform - ste!

chris:
damn - i´m going not even half as fast as i wanted

jamie:
whoa - grinding
rails is still more
fun than sex.

charles: holy shit - this guy
is even double as fast as
i thought he would go

andrea: oh boy -
i´m getting kinda horny
seeing this guy´s
sweaty armpits

goof:
i don´t understand anything...
and where is that foo...

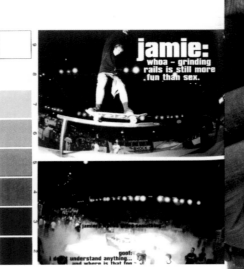

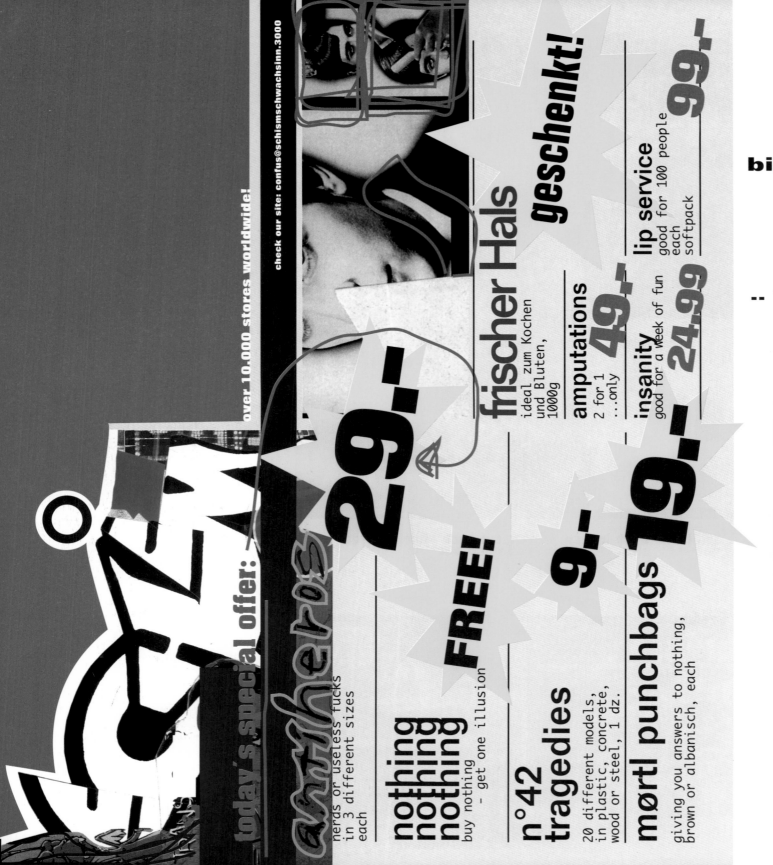

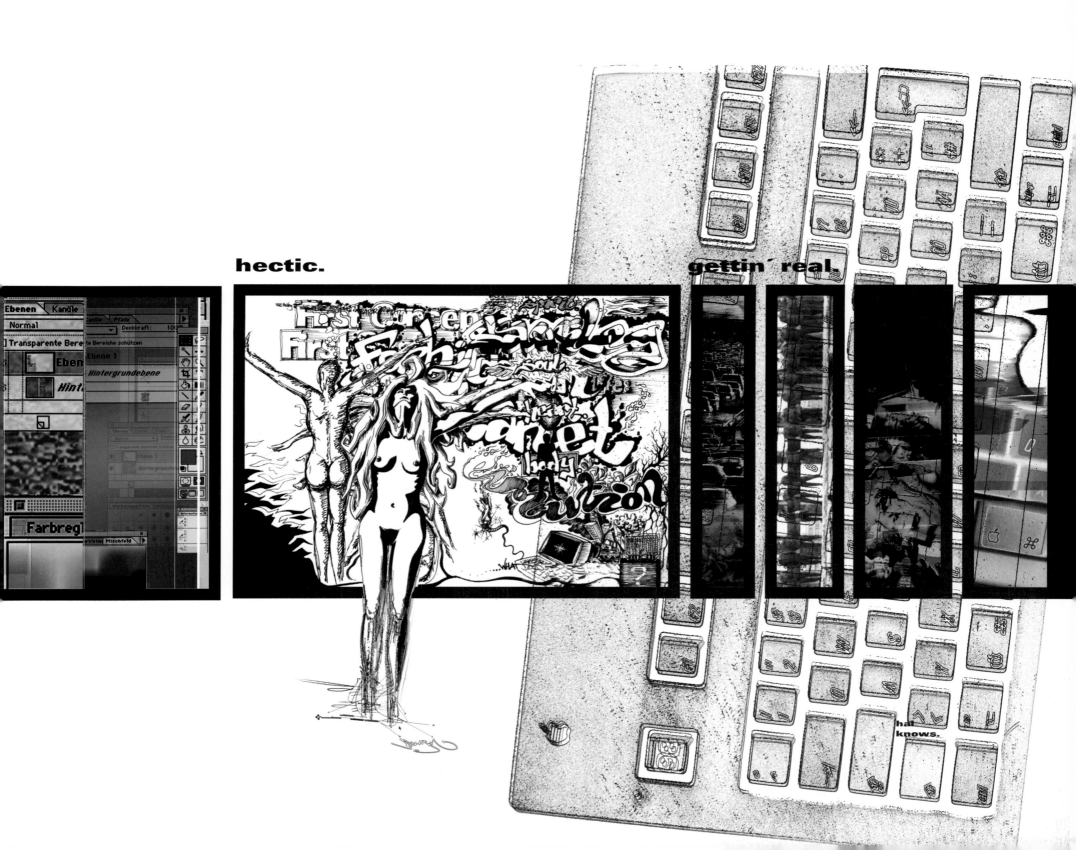

hectic.

gettin´real.

umd

beckna. sexuel obsessed teammate

umd. euroamerican urbanicoutdoor clothingcompany. fax paper to: +49 30 265 1982

How fast must a man go to get from where

GOGO starring the antagonist DOWNHILLRACER "SUPERLO8" a man who plays it cool to find out about life and love...

umd

gogo won't drop. don't be afraid. if you don't want to fall, you won't fall. it's all about strength & consciousness. m. is for mad

umd.

breakin'throughstupidcitymechanismsfindyourtruespirit.thisain'tbullshit u. is for urban

boarding thrills entertainment

opposite page: a selection of umd, owned by marok, adverts featuring **gogo & beckna**
this page: lodown coverpage of no. 6 and no. 3 featuring **steve gruber and gogo**

f.l.t.r.: **flori möhrlein** inside & outside cover no.10 by
chris stadler's optic tools,
friedl kolar and beckna at the summercamps
small pic: **the palm** at kaunertal 96 by a.d.

beckna die ten eberiarier auderuiber vx. une . winner of medcily . beals, vox 'n' beals .

beckna, sporting a vans and an umd advert in 97

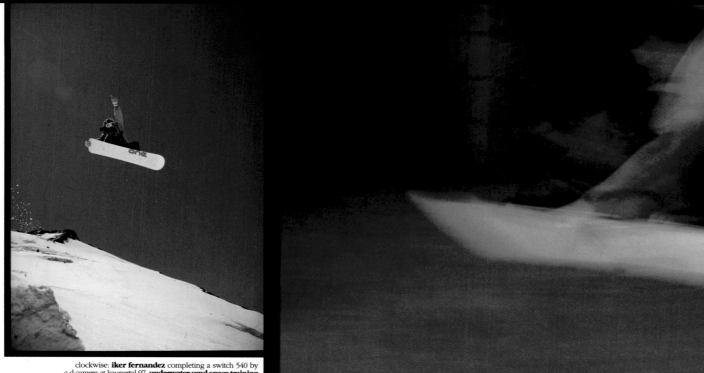

clockwise: **iker fernandez** completing a switch 540 by
a.d.camera at kaunertal 97, **underwater umd space training
camp** in 95 captured by lt. plewinski, **summercamp
tourbus** of 96, **marok** at the summercamps in 96
next page: the halfpipe in laax in 96, gogo & beckna chillin'
with that phat ol' blunt in 95.

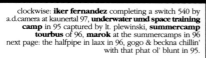

escape the city limits by richie walch

christian rüf indys over st. moritz, suisse

marius sommer enjoying some media penetration in les diablores

marius sommer at zugspitze

oli holzmann, mike basich & noah brandon, salt lake city

largest

the legendary session at riksgransen in 97, featuring the largest method 180 ever seen to man by **ingemar backmann,** so far...

ethan anderson design for volcom

andyhowell@home.com

ANDYHOWELL

Hello,
my name is Andy...
I was born on the
east coast,
but now I chill in Cali.
I live with my girlfriend
Erin, who I'll
probably marry someday.
My friends at Lodown
said, 'Bust a couple of pages,
tell us what's up!'
So I was like, 'Cool...'
And so...here I am.
Dig it, and if you want,
email me some
cool shit...,
what do I talk about,
uh...I started drawing and
painting when I was about 3
or 4 years old...

well, I guess I'll
just spit what I've been up to
since then...

*Chronology > 84-89/sponsored am > 89/turned pro > 90/co-created New Deal (skated pro / graphics, ads, clothing, video design) > 92/created Element (skated pro / graphics, ads, clothing, video design) > 93/co-created 411 Video Mag (art) > 93/created Sophisto (graphics, ads, clothing, video design) > 94/created Girly Things (graphics, ads, clothing, video design) > 95/created MTN Snow (graphics, ads, clothing, outerwear design) > 96/co-created First Bureau of Imagery (graphics, ads, clothing, packaging, fabric design) > 97/Art Direction Freeworld Entertainment NYC (created corporate identity, record sleeves, ads, posters, stickers design) > 98/art director Rowdy.Entertainment ATL (art director, record sleeves, ads, posters, stickers, clothing, video design) > 98/co-creator co-owner Rowdy.Industries (merchandising products / entertainment design / childrens publishing and music with Dallas Austin) > 98/Tornado Wheel Co (art direction, graphics, ads) > 98/Vans (snow boot/clothing ad campaigns 98/99) > 98/Coca-Cola (p.o.p. display design for Slurpee USA) > 98/New Balance (t-shirt design for 99) >>*Other highlights > 85/hanging with mark gonzales at Marty's house for a week, and he taught me how to do real ollies on street (inspiring) > 89-90/Cadillac Tour with friends Natas, Jim Thiebaud, Julien, Micke Reyes, Alan Peterson (20 days of madness and fun skating) > 90/hanging in NYC with Jeremy H, Felix, Harold, Rod, Bruno and the Shut boys (and thereafter for 3 summers), 91/touring Portugal, Spain, Switzerland, Austria, Greece, England, Japan, Hong Kong, Hawaii with Rick Iba and Justin > 89-94/countless other amazing tours > 93/being in the movie City Hunter with Jackie Chan (and hi-fi Hong Kong madness with Jose) > 89-94/pro video parts (SchmittCamp 89, New Deal promo 90, *useless wooden toys 91, #1281 92 , Element promo 92, Skypager 93, contest videos 89-92, Quiet Storm 92) > 91/pro spotlight Poweredge magazine > 92/pro spotlight Transworld Skateboarding magazine > 94/USC School of Cinema and Television requesting use of my and Ted Newsome's Freedom video for classroom study > 95/best womenswear designer award Girly Things (UHF magazine) > 95/Spin Magazine cover Kim Deal wearing a Girly Things shirt > 95/Naomi Campbell wearing Girly Things shirt in mag and video promotion of Spike Lee's Girl 6 movie > 96/Juror's Choice Award for my painting "Tough Luck, Eddie..." which I gave to my boy Damon Way > 98/writing my first childrens book with my friend Dallas doing music for an accompanying CD >>>

(well, it's been dope so far...)

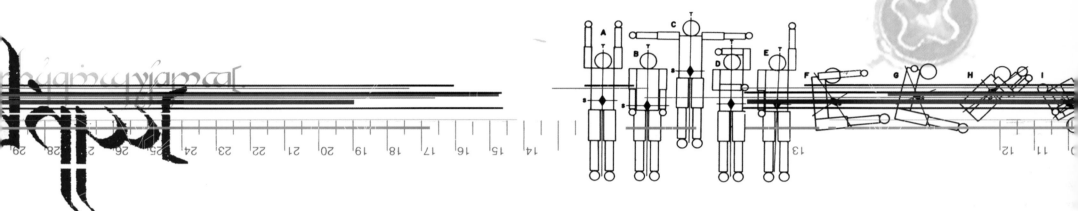

andy howell

FRONT LEFT CHEST PRINT
SOPHISTO M4-N SNAP JACKET SCREEN
3 COLOR COMBOS
MAIN LARGE PRINT BACK UPPER MIDDLE. SMALL PRINT FRONT LE'

SOPHISTO

TORNADO

GIRLY THINGS

andy howell's fine art

'sabrina lunch'

'deluxe hair flip'

'excuse me, miss lu...'

phil frost a 25 year-old brooklyn based painter extraordinary

JULI FREITAG
JULY FRIDAY
JUILLET VENDREDI

11

SOL MBAS ANO

b/w pics by jelle waagna
streetinstallationpics by mike mills
galleryshots by cheryl dunn
panoramapics by ezel

Multicolored vivacious city of San Francisco - an environment that keeps your mind awake. Evan Hecox names this surrounding as his biggest influence; the urban everyday street life.
While studying arts at the Colorado State University he already started designing clothes and sunglasses for the legendary Twist Snowboard Company, and worked there for four years in a row. Today the twentysomething is a self-employed freelancer, draws and designs for skateboardbrands, clothes, boards and videocovers. Mainly for Chocolate Skateboards, Switch Bindingsystems, and even for the TDK Audiotapes Company. Many of his unique illustrations were printed in mags' like Big Brother, Blunt, Transworld Snowboarding/Skateboarding and Lodown Magazine of course...

evan hecox

GUY MARIANO INTERVIEW

LEWIS

TWIST

SUNGLASSES

twist

1/20

20TH ST

lodown graphic engineering
by thomas marecki aka marok
& alex flach aka flachfotografics

contributers:
eddie otchere (photography)
schism (graphic design)
orel (graphic design)
marley maciek (hook ups)
götz werner (texts and phrases)
anderas hesse (textdocumentary)
richard walch (photography)
a.d. camera (photography)
oliver wia (photography)
marc lehmann (photography)
black market (graphic design)
andy howell (graphic design, fine art)
jose gomez (graphic design)
futura (fine art)
haze (graphic design)
phil frost (fine art)
evan hecox (fine art)
dimitry elyashkevich (photography)
thomas campbell (photography)
sven hagolani (photography)
and many others

thanks a lot to all creative people who made
this whole thing possible.

peace in 98,
suckers to the side...

the new world plan rises from the
underground.
unknown territories will be conquered
anyway.

lodown magazine
lützowstrasse 68
10785 berlin, germany

tel. 030 265 2096
fax 030 265 1982
lodown@lodown.de / marok@lodown.de

LODOWN graphic engineering